Laura Jackson and **Yoko Kobayashi**
Translation

Jen Quick
Retouch and Lettering

Vanessa Satone
Designer

Stephen Pakula
Production Manager

Mike Lackey
Director of Print Production

Stephanie Shalofsky
Vice President, Production

John O'Donnell
Publisher

Duck Prince Book 1: Transformation. Published
by CPM Manga, a division of Central Park
Media Corporation. Office of Publication – 250
West 57th Street, Suite 317, New York, NY
10107. Original Japanese version "Duck
Prince Book 1" © AI MORINAGA 2001.
Originally published in Japan in 2001 by
KADOKAWA SHOTEN PUBLISHING
Co.,Ltd.. English translation rights
arranged with KADOKAWA
SHOTEN PUBLISHING Co.,Ltd.,
Tokyo through TOHAN CORPO-
RATION, TOKYO. English ver-
sion © 2003 Central Park Media
Corporation. CPM Manga and
logo are registered trade-
marks of Central Park
Media Corporation.
Original Manga and
logo are trademarks
of Central Park
Media Corporation. All rights
reserved. Price per copy $9.99,
price in Canada may vary.
ISBN: 1-58664-931-0.
Catalog number: CMX
65201G. UPC: 7-
19987-00652-2-
00111. Printed in
Canada.

Contents

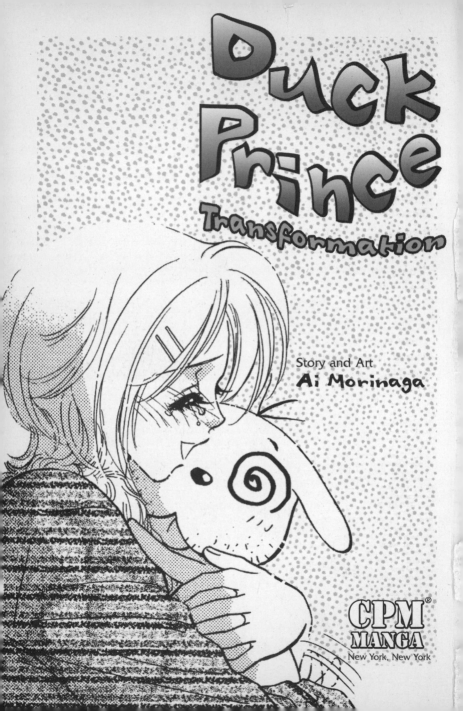

Duck Prince
Transformation

Story and Art
Ai Morinaga

CPM®
MANGA
New York, New York

Character Profiles

Reiichi

A kind hearted boy trapped in the body of a short, fat nerd who gets no respect from anybody. But things are about to change when a freak accident transforms Reiichi into something different – a handsome and charming young man who is adored by all!

before

after

Yumiko

A beautiful girl that likes Reiichi for who he truly is, and not for what he looks like. When Reiichi transforms into a handsome man, will her feelings change at all?

Evil Sisters

Reiichi's sisters act like typical older siblings... except they really don't like their little brother!

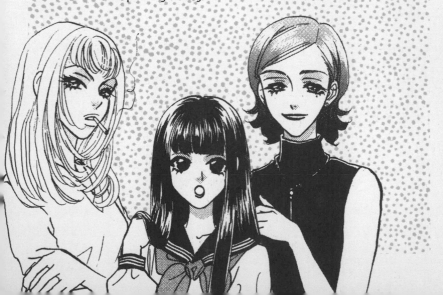

WHEN THE DUCKLING CAUGHT A GLIMPSE OF HIS REFLECTION IN THE WATER, HE WAS STUNNED.
IN AN INSTANT, THE UGLY GREY DUCKLING HAD TRANSFORMED INTO A BEAUTIFUL SWAN.

EPISODE
1

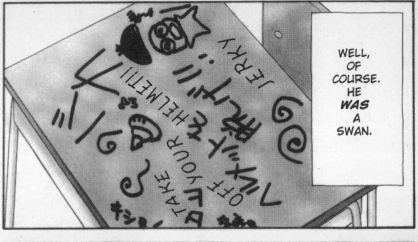

WELL, OF COURSE. HE **WAS** A SWAN.

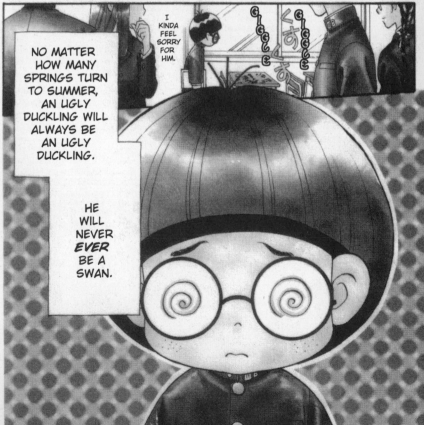

NO MATTER HOW MANY SPRINGS TURN TO SUMMER, AN UGLY DUCKLING WILL ALWAYS BE AN UGLY DUCKLING.

HE WILL NEVER **EVER** BE A SWAN.

I KINDA FEEL SORRY FOR HIM.

YOU GUYS ARE IN THE SAME BOAT. YOU OUGHTA TRY DEFENDING HIM.
EHHH?
wipe wipe
bing
INK REM-OVER
YOU GEEKS SHOULDN'T JUDGE A BOOK BY ITS COVER.
TMP
DON'T BE COMPARING US WITH SWAN.
EHH? GEEKS HAVE A HIERARCHY?
FROM WHERE WE'RE STANDING, YOU ALL LOOK THE SAME.
HMPH. THAT'S 'CAUSE YOU DON'T KNOW NOTHIN'. PAMPEE. (CHUCKLE)
PAMPEE? ARE YOU GUYS COME-DIANS?
SHIVER
...ALL I LIKE IS GREAT PLAYS AND PLANTS.
A DOG OF FLANDERS
AM I REALLY THAT BAD?
WRITING MAT
WHAAAT-EVER. A GEEK'S A GEEK.
TONNNK

WACK WACK
OH MAN! TALKING TO THESE CREEPY CHICKS IS MAKIN' ME MISS MY SAKURATAN RERUN.
OW!
WHO'RE YOU CALLING CREEPY!?
YOU'RE IN YOUR THIRD YEAR OF JUNIOR HIGH AND YOU'RE STILL WATCHING SAKURATAN!! GROSS!
THAP
(NUCLEAR EXPLOSION)
THUD
YOU ... UH... DROPPED THIS.
<BLUSH>
NOOOOO! MY NAIL FELL OFF!
I CAN'T BELIEVE IT. WHY DID YOU HAVE TO PICK IT UP!?
NOW I CAN'T WEAR IT ANYMORE.
OH MAN. I LIKED THAT ONE.
WHAT TOTAL NERDS!
COME ON, LET'S GO!!
BOOOOOO
UHH ... UHH.

UHHH... WHAT IF YOU TAPE IT?
IDIOT!
GROSS. YOU *TOUCHED* IT, HELMET.
JUST CHUCK IT.
MUST'VE BEEN EXPENSIVE.
WHAT A WASTE.
YOU BETTER GO TO THE NAIL SALON AND HAVE 'EM PUT ON A NEW ONE.
WHY...
WHY WASN'T I BORN *NORMAL*?
I'M SHORT.
I'M UGLY. MY HAIR'S THICK AND COARSE.
THOING
OUCH.
I CAN'T EVEN SEE MY OWN FACE IN THE MIRROR WITHOUT GLASSES.
BLUR

SIGH...

PLANTS ARE THE BEST.

EVEN THOUGH I'M UGLY, IF I REMEMBER TO TALK TO THEM, THEY GROW INTO BEAUTIFUL FLOWERS. *THEY* DON'T HATE ME.

GLOOOM

WOOOW! HOW BEAUTIFUL!

NICE JOB, *REIICHI.*

YUMIKO ...
HEY... WHAT'S THAT ONE CALLED?
IT... IT'S SAFFRON.
EHHH? THE SAME SAFFRON WE USE FOR COOKING?
UHH ... YEAH .
THEY USE THE STAMEN FOR FOOD COLORING.
AND THE PLANT IS USED AS A SEDATIVE AND A BRACER.
TUP うんちく
TUP うんちく
WOW!
I'M IMPRESSED! YOU KNOW EVERYTHING, REIICHI SWAN!
CLAP ぱち
CLAP ぱち
I...I JUST LIKE PLANTS. THAT'S ALL.
TEHEE. えへへ
I BET THEY KNOW YOU LIKE THEM TOO.
THAT'S WHY THEY MAKE BEAUTIFUL FLOWERS FOR YOU.

BLUUUUSH
THEY REALLY ARE BEAU-TIFUL.
I SHOULD'VE JOINED THE GARDEN CLUB INSTEAD OF GOING TO CRAM SCHOOL.
UHHH ... WOULD YOU LIKE ONE?
REALLY !?
I'LL PUT ONE IN A POT AND GIVE IT TO YOU NEXT TIME I SEE YOU.
EEEEE! THAAANK YOU!
YAAAY
YUMIKO, YOU'RE GONNA BE LATE FOR CRAM SCHOOL.
I'M COM-ING.
SEE YA LATER, REIICHI!
YOU BETTER QUIT HANGIN' AROUND HELMET, OR PEOPLE ARE GONNA START PICKING ON YOU.
OH, IT'S ALL RIGHT.
YUMIKO, YOU'RE TOO PRETTY TO BE HANGING OUT WITH A GEEK LIKE THAT.

I THINK REIICHI IS ADORABLE.
HUUUUH?
HE'S NOT A GEEK.
I THINK REIICHI IS ADORABLE.

© IWASHIMIZU
YUMIKO! I WOULD DIE FOR YOU!!!
POP
th-thump th-thump th-thump
AHHH. YUMIKO...
ADORABLE? ME?
sigh

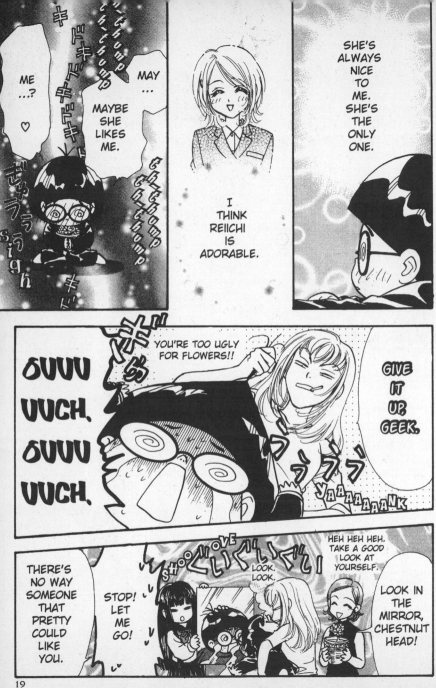

ME...?

♡

MAY...

MAYBE SHE LIKES ME.

chchomp chchomp chchomp

sigh

I THINK REIICHI IS ADORABLE.

SHE'S ALWAYS NICE TO ME. SHE'S THE ONLY ONE.

YOU'RE TOO UGLY FOR FLOWERS!!

GIVE IT UP, GEEK.

SVUU VUCH.

SVUU VUCH.

YAAAAAAANK

THERE'S NO WAY SOMEONE THAT PRETTY COULD LIKE YOU.

STOP! LET ME GO!

SHOVE

LOOK. LOOK.

HEH HEH HEH. TAKE A GOOD LOOK AT YOURSELF.

LOOK IN THE MIRROR, CHESTNUT HEAD!

19

SHE PITIES YOU ... PITY.
P-I-T-Y!
A GIRL LIKE THAT IS NICE TO BUGS!
RIP RIP RIP RIP
HOW COULD YOU HANG UP SOMETHING LIKE THIS? YOU GROSS ME OUT, NERD!
I GUESS EVEN INSECTS AND WORMS HAVE A SURVIVAL INSTINCT.
HEY, CAN'T YOU DO SOMETHING ABOUT THE WAY YOU LOOK?
IT'S TOTALLY EMBARRASSING WHEN PEOPLE FIND OUT YOU'RE OUR BROTHER.
TRUE.

IF YOU LIKE SOMEONE, YOU OUGHTA TRY TO LOOK GOOD FOR THEM.
BUT I CAN'T DO ANYTHING ABOUT MY COARSE HAIR AND I CAN'T WEAR CONTACTS 'CAUSE THEY HURT TOO MUCH.
QUIT MAKING EXCUSES!
YOU'RE NOT TRYING HARD ENOUGH.
WACK
YOU'RE ACTING LIKE A BEATEN DOWN DOG!
SNAP
YOU'RE NOT EVEN A GOOD NERD.
<cough>
HOW WOULD YOU LIKE IT--
--IF YOU WERE THE ONLY UGLY ONE?
THAT'S NOT SOMETHING WE NEED TO THINK ABOUT.
WE'RE BEAU-TIFUL.
WACK
KRhh
YUMIKO MUST BE A SAINT.
I CAN'T EVEN STAND TO BE NEAR HIM.
HMM. MAYBE SHE JUST FEELS SORRY FOR HIM LIKE SHE WOULD A MANGY STRAY DOG.

YUMIKO IS DIFFERENT FROM YOU GUYS!
HEY, REIICHI.
TOK
bonk
HE'S A WORM. HE'S REALLY A WORM.
HEY.
MY KELLY BAG.
YUMIKO IS...
YUMIKO IS THE ONLY ONE...
WOOOW!

THANK YOU, REIICHI!
にっお
GRIN
きゅうん
TH...TH... THESE ARE THE INSTRUCTIONS FOR TAKING CARE OF IT.
OOOH! I'M SO HAPPY! I'M GONNA TAKE REAL GOOD CARE OF IT.
IF YOU HAVE ANY QUESTIONS, PLEASE ASK.
INSTRUCTIONS
I DON'T MIND NOT BEING ABLE TO TELL HER I LIKE HER.
IT'S ENOUGH JUST BEING NEAR HER AND SEEING HER SMILING FACE ONCE IN A WHILE.
WOW! HOW PRETTY!

TOO...
WOBBLE
TOO UGLY!!
I CAN'T EVEN STAND TO BE NEAR HIM.
HUH?
WHAT'S WRONG, REIICHI?
ST... STOP. DON'T COME ANY CLOSER.
BEING NEAR HER...

WHY NOT?
'CAUSE... 'CAUSE I'M UGLY.
IF PEOPLE SEE YOU WITH ME, THEY'RE GONNA LAUGH AT YOU.
WOOZE WOOZE
OHHHH, THAT'S NOT TRUE.
YOU'RE CUTE, REIICHI! ♡
IT'S OKAY.
YOU DON'T HAVE TO PITY ME. I KNOW I'M UGLY.
I MEAN IT!
YOU ARE CUTE. ACT-UALLY ...
HUH?
ACTUALLY?
TEE HEE. IT'S A SECRET. ♡
BLUSH
SHE'S BLUSH -ING ?

NO WAAAAY! SHE REALLY DOES LIKE ME!
YAH. YUMIKO REALLY IS DIFFERENT FROM MY SISTERS AND THEIR FRIENDS.
YUMIKO IS DIFFERENT !!
YUMIKO...
WAAAH.

AHHH, MISTER!
boing
ぴよ
squat
ひょい
HUFF HUFF
WHAT'S UP? DID YOU COME ALL THIS WAY TO FIND ME?
YOU KNOW THE WAY TO SCHOOL?
AND I ONLY WALKED YOU HERE ONCE!
bonk
HUFF HUFF
MY-HEAD-OUUUUCH.
あーたーまーがああぁ
?
HUFF HUFF
WHAT HAPPENED, REIICHI?
spurt spurt
Flop Flop Flop Flop
UHHH.
NOTHING.
BING
ぎくっ

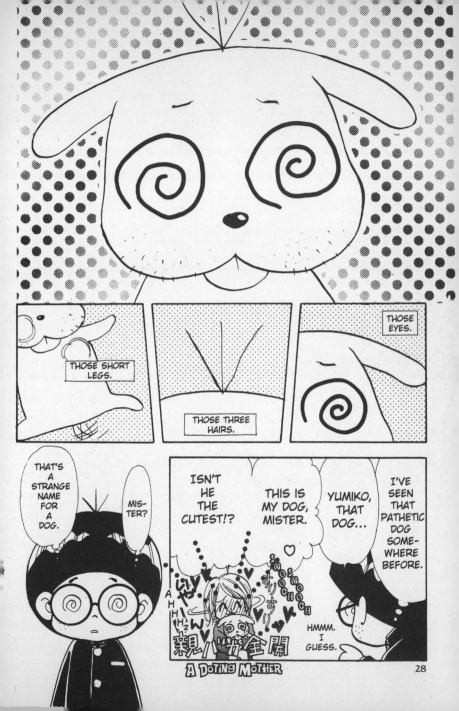

THOSE EYES.

THOSE SHORT LEGS.

THOSE THREE HAIRS.

THAT'S A STRANGE NAME FOR A DOG.

MIS-TER?

ISN'T HE THE CUTEST!?

THIS IS MY DOG, MISTER.

YUMIKO, THAT DOG...

I'VE SEEN THAT PATHETIC DOG SOME-WHERE BEFORE.

HMMM. I GUESS.

A DOTING MOTHER

28

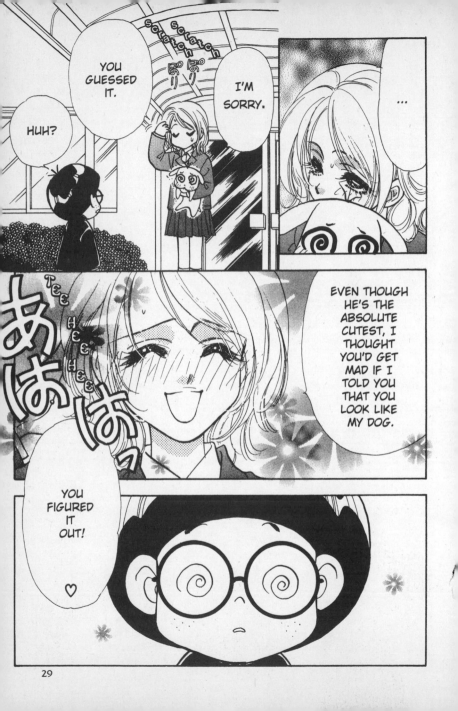

...
I'M SORRY.
scratch scratch
ぽり ぽり
YOU GUESSED IT.
HUH?
EVEN THOUGH HE'S THE ABSOLUTE CUTEST, I THOUGHT YOU'D GET MAD IF I TOLD YOU THAT YOU LOOK LIKE MY DOG.
TEE HEE HEE
あははっ
YOU FIGURED IT OUT!
♥

犬(いぬ)——!!?
A dog…!!?
ガラガラ
ガラガラ
BWWOOO…

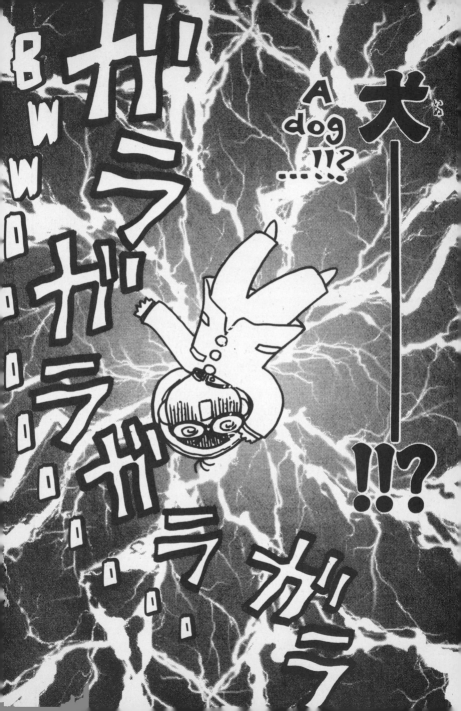

RRRUFF
RRRUFF
MISTER?
WHAT'S WRONG?
MISTER...
GLOOOOM
sniff
NO, MISTER WAS NAMED AFTER ME!
sniff
sniff
HE HASN'T GONE TO SCHOOL FOR TEN DAYS. IT'S STARTING TO FEEL LIKE A MORGUE IN HERE.
sniff
sniff
HMMM. I WONDER WHAT'S WRONG WITH HIM. MAYBE HE'S DEPRESSED.
sniff
sniff

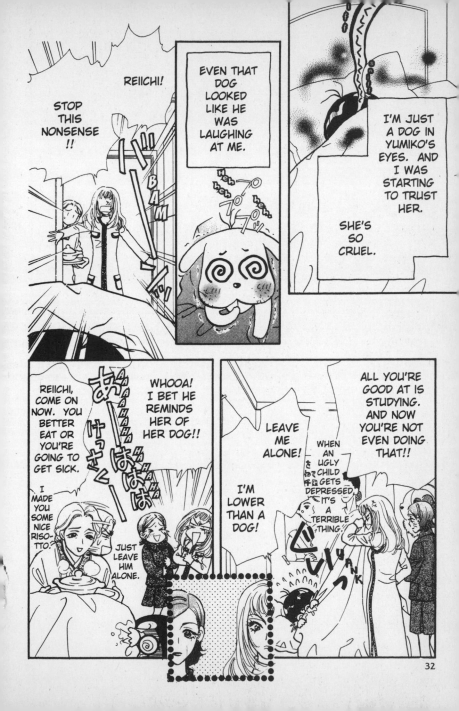

REIICHI!

STOP THIS NONSENSE!!

EVEN THAT DOG LOOKED LIKE HE WAS LAUGHING AT ME.

Heh Heh Heh Heh!

BAM

I'M JUST A DOG IN YUMIKO'S EYES. AND I WAS STARTING TO TRUST HER.

SHE'S SO CRUEL.

REIICHI, COME ON NOW. YOU BETTER EAT OR YOU'RE GOING TO GET SICK.

I MADE YOU SOME NICE RISOTTO.

JUST LEAVE HIM ALONE.

WHOOA! I BET HE REMINDS HER OF HER DOG!!

LEAVE ME ALONE!

I'M LOWER THAN A DOG!

WHEN AN UGLY CHILD GETS DEPRESSED IT'S A TERRIBLE THING.

ALL YOU'RE GOOD AT IS STUDYING. AND NOW YOU'RE NOT EVEN DOING THAT!!

YANK

32

sniff
sniff
sniff
sniff
I DON'T WANT IT. I WANNA DIE.
THEN MAYBE I'LL BE REINCARNATED AS A BEAUTIFUL PERSON.
YAAANK
Aaiee..
HOW DARE YOU SAY THAT!?
UHH.
UHHH.
DO YOU KNOW WHAT IT WAS LIKE GIVING BIRTH TO YOU!?
WITH YOUR SCRAWNY BODY AND GIANT HEAD.
I HAD TO STRAIN SO HARD TO GET YOU OUT. I NEARLY DIED WITH YOU STUCK BETWEEN MY LEGS!
UHHH ... MOM ...

I RISKED MY LIFE GIVING BIRTH TO YOU, SO DON'T SAY YOU WANT TO DIE JUST BECAUSE YOU'RE UGLY!!
YOU STRETCHED ME ALL OUT OF SHAPE!
WAAAAAAAH.
NOW GET OUT OF THAT BED AND GO TO SCHOOL!
HUP
O... OKAY...
AHHH...
trudge trudge
I DON'T WANNA GO TO SCHOOL.
I DON'T WANNA SEE YUMIKO.
WHAT IF I SEE HER? WHAT AM I GONNA DO?
...
MORNING.
Whhip

HEY, IT'S HELMET!
ZZZZing
HEY, WHERE'VE YOU BEEN?
UHH ...
UHHH.
YUMIKO WANTED TO SAY GOOD-BYE.
EH?
zing
SAY ... GOOD-BYE?
OH, YOU DIDN'T KNOW?
YUMIKO'S DAD WAS TRANSFERRED TO AMERICA.
HER WHOLE FAMILY'S MOVING THERE. YESTERDAY WAS HER LAST DAY.

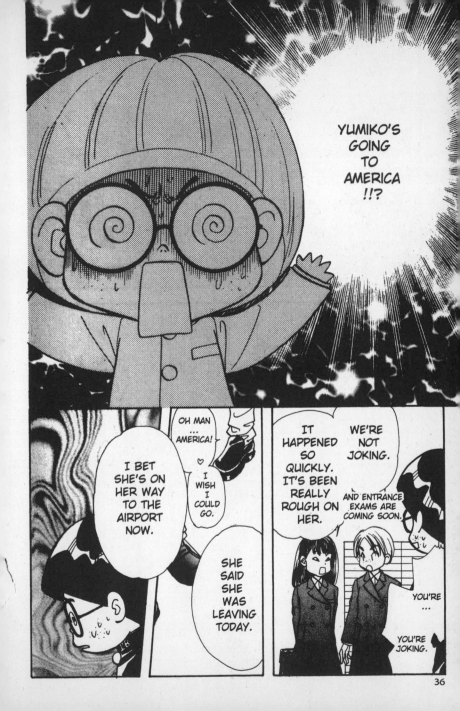

YUMIKO'S GOING TO AMERICA!!?

OH MAN... AMERICA!

I WISH I COULD GO.

I BET SHE'S ON HER WAY TO THE AIRPORT NOW.

SHE SAID SHE WAS LEAVING TODAY.

IT HAPPENED SO QUICKLY. IT'S BEEN REALLY ROUGH ON HER.

WE'RE NOT JOKING.

AND ENTRANCE EXAMS ARE COMING SOON.

YOU'RE... YOU'RE JOKING.

YUMIKO!
HUH? HELMET?
HEY...ARE YOU CUTTING CLASS AGAIN!?
I'M SORRY.
I SAID I DIDN'T WANT TO SEE HER, BUT THAT WAS A LIE.
I DON'T CARE IF SHE THINKS I'M A DOG. I NEED TO SEE HER.
I CAN'T GO WITHOUT SEEING HER AGAIN.
IT'S THAT WAY.
I ABSOLUTELY CAN'T.

YU...
YUMIIIKO.
わああああ
waaaa
I MADE IT!
REIICHI !?
YOU GOTTA HELP ME FIND MISTER!!
MAYBE HE'LL COME OUT IF HE SEES YOU!
EH?
MISTER IS MISSING.
AND WE'RE LEAVING FOR THE AIRPORT REAL SOON.
うわああああ
uwwwwahhh
ブラ〜ン
dangle~
IF WE DON'T FIND HIM QUICK, HE'LL BE LEFT BEHIND!
YU... YUMIKO.

sniff ぐす…
YUMIKO IS CRYING.
ひくっ hic
I'LL HELP YOU LOOK. WE'LL FIND HIM.
I PROMISE!
MY BELOVED YUMIKO.
UHH. I'LL LOOK OVER THERE.
PLEASE HURRY, REIICHI!
I HAVE TO FIND HIM!
SO WHAT IF SHE LIKES ME 'CAUSE I LOOK LIKE HER DOG? SHE'S THE ONLY ONE WHO'S EVER BEEN NICE TO ME.
HELL-OOO.
MISTER!?
あ!! Augh!
WRONG DOG.
YUMIKO IS MY LIFE.

THIS IS THE LAST TIME I'LL SEE HER. I HAVE TO HELP HER NO MATTER WHAT.
HAVE YOU SEEN A DOG THAT LOOKS LIKE THIS?
SHOCK
!!
MISTER !?

Grrrr?

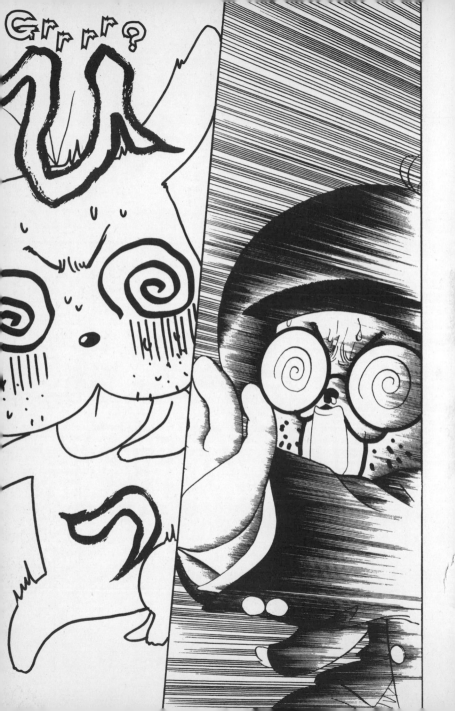

SHOOOOOOOOOOM
WHY'S HE ...?
HEY... DON'T RUN AWAY!
MISTER, WAAAIT!
TIKTIK
BEEEP
BEEEEEP

LOOK OUT !
SPLAT

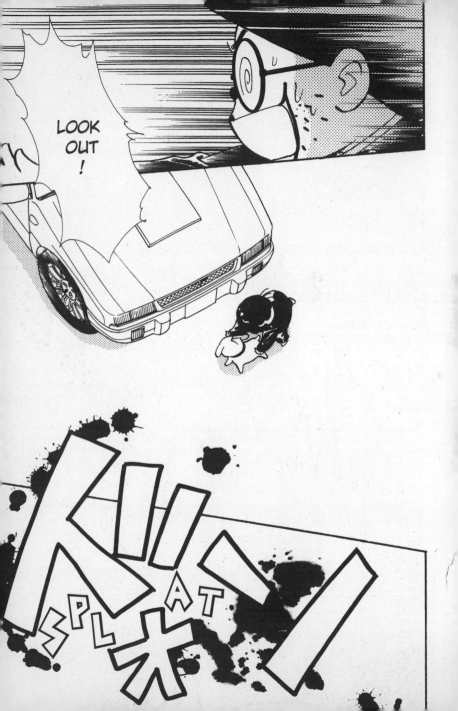

きゃー
Eeeek.
JABBER ザワ
THAT BOY JUST GOT HIT.
JABBER ザワ
CALL AN AMBULANCE!
YIP YIP.
OH, THANK GOODNESS.
MISTER'S ALIVE.
MISTER, YUMIKO'S BEEN CRYING FOR YOU.
YOU BETTER HURRY HOME.
MAYBE NOW--
--YUMIKO WILL THINK I WAS USEFUL.

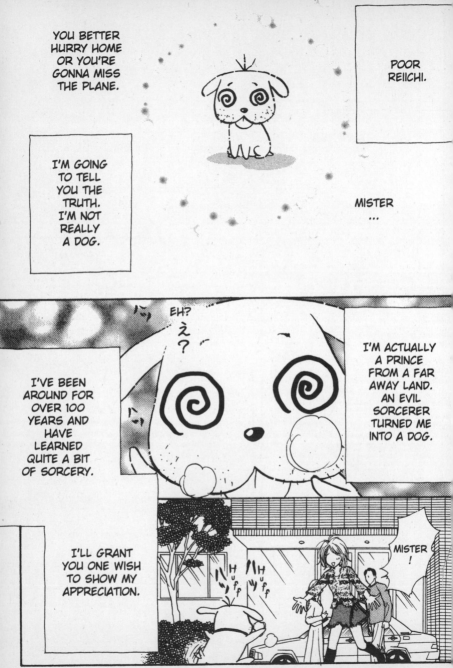

YOU BETTER HURRY HOME OR YOU'RE GONNA MISS THE PLANE.

POOR REIICHI.

I'M GOING TO TELL YOU THE TRUTH. I'M NOT REALLY A DOG.

MISTER ...

EH?
え？

I'VE BEEN AROUND FOR OVER 100 YEARS AND HAVE LEARNED QUITE A BIT OF SORCERY.

I'M ACTUALLY A PRINCE FROM A FAR AWAY LAND. AN EVIL SORCERER TURNED ME INTO A DOG.

I'LL GRANT YOU ONE WISH TO SHOW MY APPRECIATION.

MISTER !

Huff Huff

45

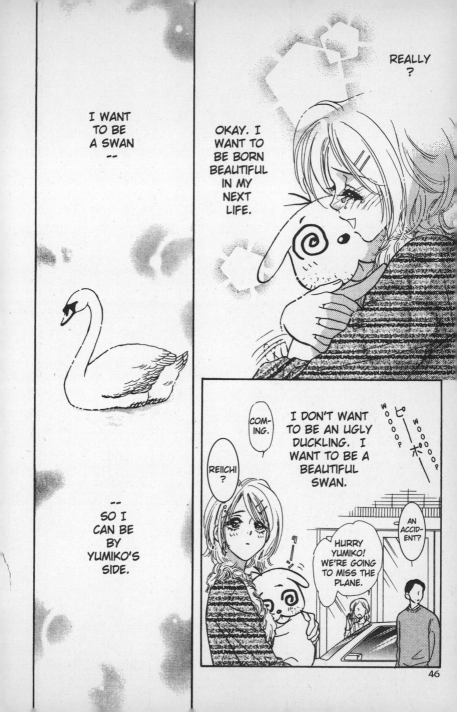

I WANT TO BE A SWAN --

-- SO I CAN BE BY YUMIKO'S SIDE.

REALLY?

OKAY. I WANT TO BE BORN BEAUTIFUL IN MY NEXT LIFE.

COMING.

REIICHI?

I DON'T WANT TO BE AN UGLY DUCKLING. I WANT TO BE A BEAUTIFUL SWAN.

HURRY YUMIKO! WE'RE GOING TO MISS THE PLANE.

AN ACCIDENT?

WOOOOP

WOOOOP

NNNGH.
WHAT A STRANGE DREAM.

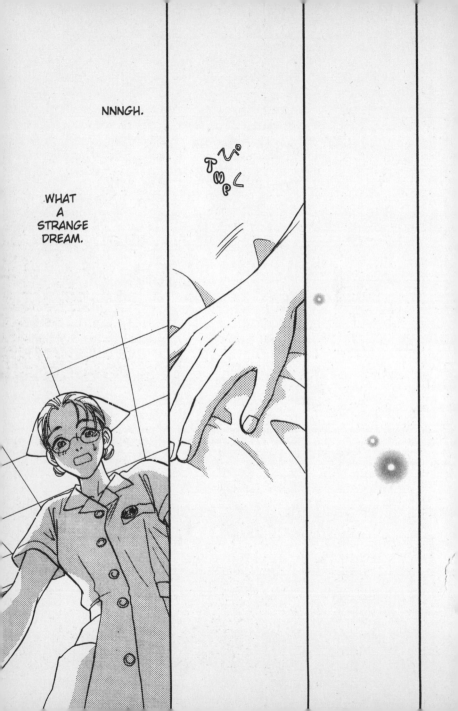

SHIRO HOSPITAL
大城総合病院
WHY WOULD I HAVE A DREAM LIKE THAT?
DOC …
DOCTOR, REIICHI IS COMING BACK!!
バタバタ
flap flap
DAD
父
OHHH. THANK HEAVENS. REIICHI!
YOU'VE BEEN UNCONSCIOUS FOR A YEAR.
DO YOU REMEMBER THE ACCIDENT?
ONE … ONE YEAR?
YEP. WE THOUGHT YOU WOULD NEVER COME TO.

OH YEAH, IT'S BEEN A WHOLE YEAR SINCE...
THEY SAY YOU WERE WITH A DOG WHEN YOU GOT HIT, BUT THE DOG DISAPPEARED.
RIGHT ...
I WONDER IF MISTER MADE IT BACK TO YUMIKO.
ALL MOM'S DONE SINCE IT HAPPENED IS CRY.
AH ...
MY BOY IS BACK.
EVERY-THING'S FINE NOW.
WE WERE SO LUCKY TO GET THE DOCTOR WE HAD! ♡
SIGH
I THINK IT WAS AN ACT OF GOD! ♡
HUH ?
IS SOMETHING COVERING MY FACE?
EH?

WHO IS THAT?
IT'S YOU, YOU IDIOT!
I GUESS YOU HAVEN'T CHANGED ON THE INSIDE.
FWIP
REIICHI! YOU CAN'T WALK YET!
Aaiee.
FWOP
OUCH.
WACK
CRAWLING

YOU HIT THE WINDSHIELD AND YOUR FACE GOT ALL MESSED UP.
THE PLASTIC SURGEON HAD QUITE A JOB TO DO.
WE TOLD HIM NOT TO RESTORE YOUR OLD FACE, BUT TO MAKE YOU BEAUTIFUL INSTEAD.
YEAH!
AND WE PAID PLENTY FOR IT.
あははっ
Ahhhhahhahahah
N...
NOOOOO.

BUT THE DOCTOR WAS A HUMBLE MAN.
THANK YOU, DOCTOR !!
WELL...I REALLY DIDN'T DO THAT MUCH.
YAY! ♡
WOW! WHAT BEAUTIFUL EYES!
BU... BUT MY BODY...
YOU MUST'VE GOTTEN HIT IN A GOOD SPOT--
--BECAUSE YOU'VE BEEN GROWING RAPIDLY ALL YEAR.
AND THEY SAY THAT AN ACCIDENT CAN CAUSE A CHANGE IN HAIR TEXTURE, TOO.
I WANT TO BE BORN BEAUTIFUL IN MY NEXT LIFE.
MY WISH CAME TRUE !!

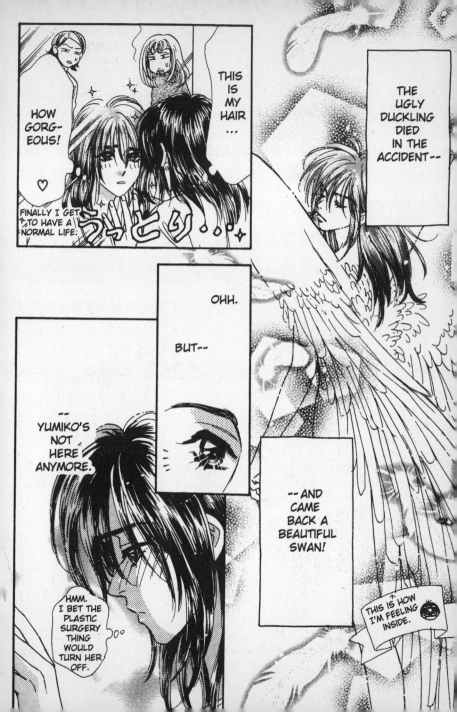

THE UGLY DUCKLING DIED IN THE ACCIDENT--

HOW GORGEOUS!

FINALLY I GET TO HAVE A NORMAL LIFE.

THIS IS MY HAIR...

らっとり...✧

OHH.

BUT--

--YUMIKO'S NOT HERE ANYMORE.

-- AND CAME BACK A BEAUTIFUL SWAN!

HMM. I BET THE PLASTIC SURGERY THING WOULD TURN HER OFF.

THIS IS HOW I'M FEELING INSIDE.

PI PI PI
REIICHI, IT'S A GOOD THING THEY LET YOU GRADUATE FROM JUNIOR HIGH AFTER YOU MISSED SO MUCH SCHOOL.
HUH? THEY DID?
BUT YOU'RE A YEAR BEHIND, AND YOU'VE GOT TWO MONTHS TO GET READY FOR HIGH SCHOOL ENTRANCE EXAMS!
HE'S A BOOKWORM. HE'LL BE FINE.
RIGHT NOW YOU'RE LIKE A FANCY SPORTS CAR WITH A USED ENGINE.
SHP
WE'VE GOTTA DO SOMETHING ABOUT YOUR INTERIOR.
WHILE YOU WERE IN A COMA, MOM GOT INTO FORTUNE TELLING AND DECIDED IT WAS BEST THAT WE MOVE.
EH?
SO IF YOU GET INTO A HIGH SCHOOL WHERE NOBODY KNOWS YOU, YOU CAN START A NEW LIFE.
YOU DON'T WANT TO BE ALL DEPRESSED LIKE BEFORE, DO YOU?
UH UH.

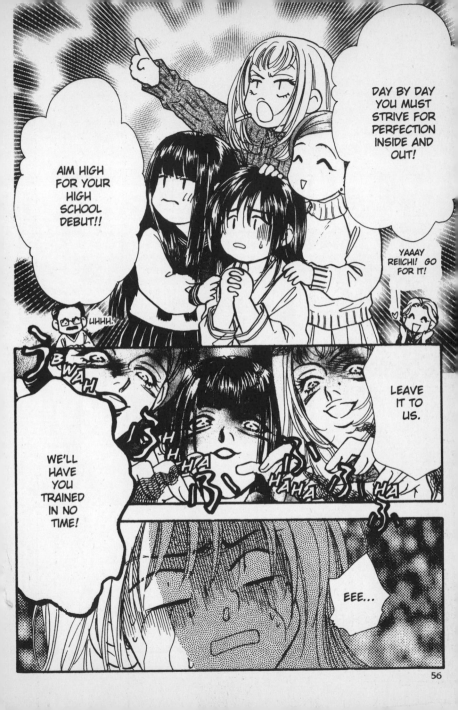

DAY BY DAY YOU MUST STRIVE FOR PERFECTION INSIDE AND OUT!

AIM HIGH FOR YOUR HIGH SCHOOL DEBUT!!

YAAAY REIICHI! GO FOR IT!

UHHH...

LEAVE IT TO US.

WE'LL HAVE YOU TRAINED IN NO TIME!

BWAH

BUHAHAHA

EEE...

EEEEEEK

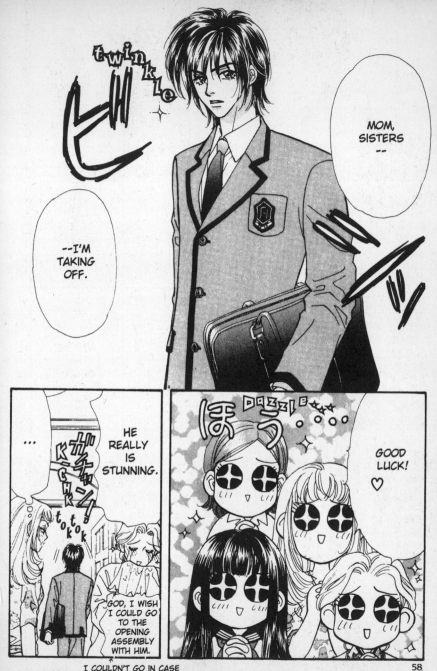

twinkle

MOM, SISTERS --

--I'M TAKING OFF.

...

HE REALLY IS STUNNING.

GOD, I WISH I COULD GO TO THE OPENING ASSEMBLY WITH HIM.

I COULDN'T GO IN CASE SOMEONE RECOGNIZED ME.

DAZZLE....

GOOD LUCK! ♥

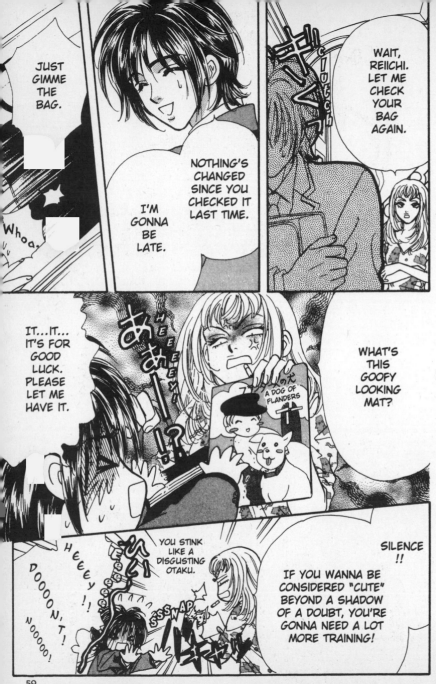

JUST GIMME THE BAG.

NOTHING'S CHANGED SINCE YOU CHECKED IT LAST TIME.

I'M GONNA BE LATE.

WAIT, REIICHI. LET ME CHECK YOUR BAG AGAIN.

Whoa.

IT...IT... IT'S FOR GOOD LUCK. PLEASE LET ME HAVE IT.

A DOG OF FLANDERS

WHAT'S THIS GOOFY LOOKING MAT?

YOU STINK LIKE A DISGUSTING OTAKU.

SILENCE!!

IF YOU WANNA BE CONSIDERED "CUTE" BEYOND A SHADOW OF A DOUBT, YOU'RE GONNA NEED A LOT MORE TRAINING!

DOOOONT! NOOOOO! SSSNAP

59

OH, WELL. LOOKS LIKE FOUR MONTHS WASN'T LONG ENOUGH.
HE'S STILL THE SAME INSIDE.
jabber jabber
DON'T LOOK DOWN WHEN YOU WALK. YOU'LL PICK UP NEGATIVE ENERGY.
ホラッ
HEY!

私立旭ヶ丘高等学校
ASAHIGAOKA HIGH SCHOOL

GULP
SO THIS IS WHERE MY NEW LIFE BEGINS.
FEELS LIKE I WAS SWEATING BLOOD DURING THAT FOUR MONTH TRAINING.
UH UHHH... DID YOU SEE LAST NIGHT'S LIL' ROMEO RERUN?
Ughh
INITIATING A CONVERSATION
HAVE CONFIDENCE, REIICHI!
Pff!
SMILE!
FASHION CHECK
I'M GOING TO TRY HARD TO HIDE MY SHORT, UGLY, HELMET PAST AND BEGIN A BRIGHT NEW SCHOOL LIFE.
HUH?
ARE...
jabber jabber
WOOOOOW.
WHOA...
ARE THEY LOOKING AT ME?
WH... WHAT SHOULD I DO?
DO I LOOK FUNNY?

ギク
STARE
シャク
STARE
ギク
STARE
Moving together.
ばたっ
THUD
し――ん
DUUUUUUUH
I CAN'T !!!
ARE YOU OKAY ?

UHHH ...
HI.
HUP
ばっ
にっこーり
GRIN
ガ
I'VE BEEN RUNNING A FEVER.

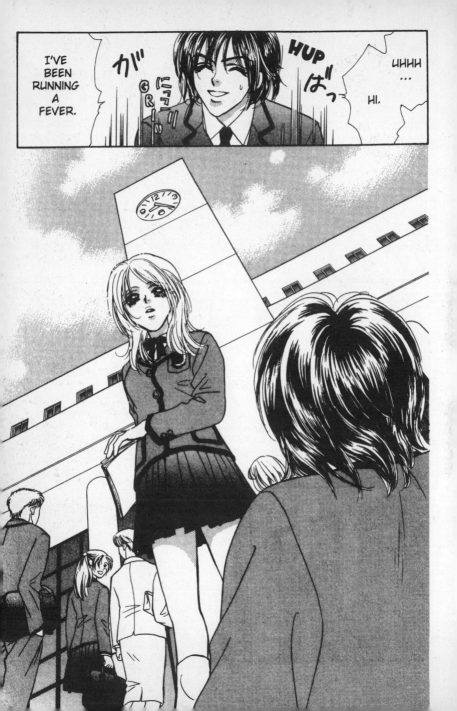

YU ...
YUMIKO !?
WHAT THE ...!?
WEREN'T ...
WEREN'T YOU IN AMERICA ?

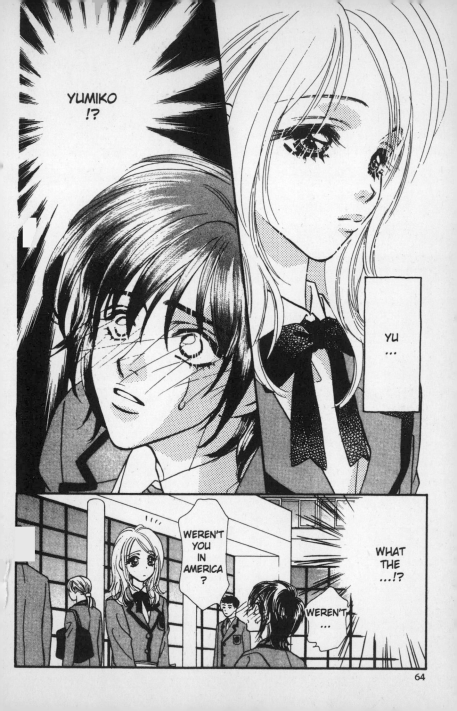

?
OOOPS !
AMERICA ?
UHH. UHHH. NEVER-MIND.
slap
IF YOU'RE NOT WELL, YOU SHOULD GO TO THE NURSE'S OFFICE.
I ...
I'M FINE.
AS A NEW STUDENT,
YOU NEED TO CHECK YOUR CLASSES ON THE BULLETIN BOARD AND GO TO YOUR FIRST PERIOD.
OKAY.
AND TAKE ONE OF THESE.
IN CASE YOU'RE INTERESTED.
GARDEN CLUB
JOIN TODAY.
ENJOY GROWING BEAUTIFUL FLOWERS WITH THE GARDEN CLUB.
CONTACT THE FOLLOWING STUDENTS TO APPLY:
3-C MAKINO
2-B ITOH
KIMURA

SEE YA AROUND! ♡
ニッコリ
GRIN
IT REALLY IS YUMIKO.
牧
B 伊藤
ITOH
浜崎
HAMASAKI
1-E
IS THIS REALLY HAPPENING?
I DON'T KNOW WHY YUMIKO'S HERE INSTEAD OF IN AMERICA,
BUT SINCE SHE'S A SECOND YEAR STUDENT AND WE'RE NOW A YEAR APART--
ご入学
WELCOME FIRST YEAR STUDENTS.

--IT MEANS WE'LL BE IN THE SAME SCHOOL FOR THE NEXT TWO YEARS.
じいん
sighhh
THIS MUST BE THE RED THREAD OF DESTINY CONNECTING US. ♡
REIICHI SWAN IS SO HANDSOME! ♡
AHHH. ♡ ♡
TEE HEE HEE
クスッ クス クス
HE'S SO MYSTERIOUS.
I CAN'T IMAGINE WHAT HE'S THINKING.
RINGGG-!
RINGGG-!
RATTLE
HEY...
REIICHI!
HAVE YOU DECIDED ON A CLUB TO JOIN?

IF YOU WANT, WE CAN GO CHECK OUT THE TENNIS CLUB TOGETHER.
UHH ...
...
じっ
stare
どきん
blink
... UHHH.
REIICHI ?
感動
BLUSH
I NEVER THOUGHT I'D SEE THE DAY THAT GIRLS IN MY CLASS WOULD TALK TO ME LIKE THIS!
REALLY ?
WHICH ONE ?
えー
SORRY.
I'VE ALREADY DECIDED ON A CLUB.

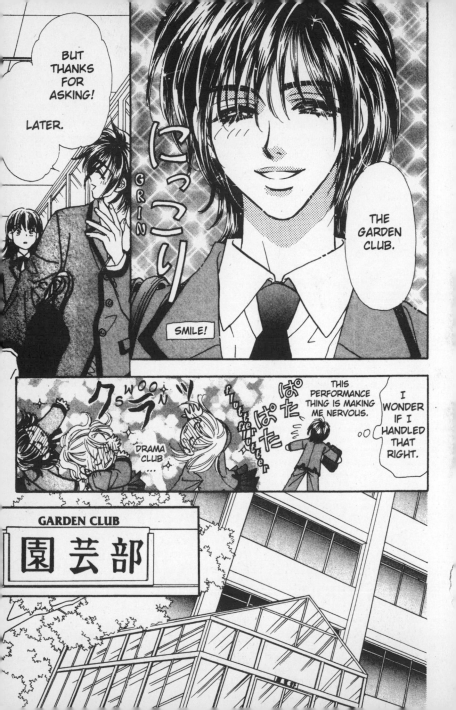

BUT THANKS FOR ASKING!

LATER.

GRIN

SMILE!

THE GARDEN CLUB.

SWOO

DRAMA CLUB...

flutter flutter

THIS PERFORMANCE THING IS MAKING ME NERVOUS.

I WONDER IF I HANDLED THAT RIGHT.

GARDEN CLUB

園芸部

WOW.
YOU'RE HERE ? ♡
UHH ...HI.
UHH... HERE.
Application
I'M LOOKING FORWARD TO THIS.
YOU'VE ALREADY DECIDED !?
DO YOU NEED PREVIOUS EXPERIENCE ?
'CAUSE I WAS IN THE GARDEN CLUB IN JUNIOR HIGH.
HEEEEH?
REALLY !?

GREEEEAT! A NEW MEMBER WITH EXPERIENCE. HOW LUCKY WE ARE?
THERE WEREN'T MANY MEMBERS TO BEGIN WITH. ♡
ACTUALLY, I JUST JOINED MYSELF, BUT I DON'T REALLY KNOW HOW TO GROW PLANTS.
I JUST TRANSFERRED HERE THIS YEAR.
WHERE WERE YOU BEFORE?
AMERICA. JUST FOR A YEAR.
MY DAD GOT ASSIGNED THERE, SO THE WHOLE FAMILY MOVED.
BUT THE COMPANY CLOSED THE U.S. BRANCH BECAUSE OF THE ECONOMIC SLUMP.
IT WAS KINDA ROUGH FOR ME 'CAUSE THAT'S WHEN EVERYONE WAS GETTING READY FOR ENTRANCE EXAMS.
OHHH. HMM.
OH, BY THE WAY, I'M YUMIKO ITOH!
IT'S REALLY NICE MEETING YOU.
AND YOU ARE --

-- SWAN.
REIICHI SWAN ?
YEP.
I DON'T THINK SHE'LL FIGURE IT OUT.
WE'RE IN DIFFERENT GRADES NOW.
WHAT A COINCIDENCE !
THERE WAS A KID IN MY CLASS IN JUNIOR HIGH WITH THE SAME NAME.
AH!
ほっ
REALLY ?
Tee hee.
えへへ
HE WAS IN THE GARDEN CLUB TOO.
HE WAS SOOO GOOD AT GROWING FLOWERS.
BLUSH
YUMIKO --
YUMIKO, I'VE BEEN REBORN.
EXCUSE ME, REIICHI.
-- DO YOU HAVE A MINUTE ?
NO PROBLEM. I'LL JUST LOOK AROUND.

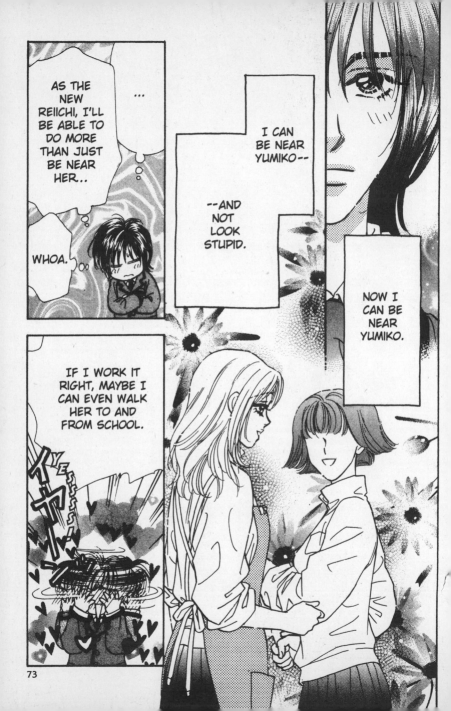

AS THE NEW REIICHI, I'LL BE ABLE TO DO MORE THAN JUST BE NEAR HER...

...

WHOA.

I CAN BE NEAR YUMIKO--

--AND NOT LOOK STUPID.

NOW I CAN BE NEAR YUMIKO.

IF I WORK IT RIGHT, MAYBE I CAN EVEN WALK HER TO AND FROM SCHOOL.

YESSS!!

THAP
NOT A CHANCE!!
SHEESH. WHAT ARE YOU DOING IN HERE?
DON'T FORGET YOU'RE REALLY HELMET.
EEEK.
pfff
AAIEE.
A PHANTOM!
YOU'RE THE PHANTOM!
WACK
SHUSH UP!!

BAM
REIICHI, WHAT HAPPENED!?
hic
Huh?
WH... WHAT...!?
BAD MISTER! WHAT ARE YOU DOING HERE!?
...
yip
yip
yip
YOU DID THIS ONCE BEFORE.
DID YOU COME TO GET ME?
huff
huff
huff
THAT WAS SWEET OF YOU, BUT YOU KNOW IT'S DANGEROUS FOR YOU TO COME OUT ALONE.
YOU'RE SOOOO CUTE!
smack
Ahhhhh?
JUST WAIT A MINUTE AND WE'LL GO HOME TOGETHER.
I'LL BE RIGHT BACK.
whimper
yip
yip
REIICHI, DO YOU MIND WATCHING THIS LITTLE GUY FOR A SEC?
whimper

THAT WAS CLOSE. THAT WAS REAL CLOSE.
whew
'CAUSE OF YOUR BIG MOUTH.
YOU ... YOU'RE ...
MISTER.
WHY'RE YOU BEING ALL SUSPICIOUS ?
WE'VE ALREADY MET.
scratch
scratch
BU... BUT THAT WAS A DREAM.
HE'S EVEN MORE DISGUSTING IN PERSON.
IT WASN'T A DREAM.
leap!
IF YOU THINK ABOUT IT, IT WOULD'VE BEEN IMPOSSIBLE TO CHANGE YOUR OLD FACE INTO THIS ONE BY PLASTIC SURGERY ALONE.
現代医学じゃムリムリ!!
MODERN MEDICINE ISN'T THAT GOOD!!
DUUUUUN.

YOU'RE THE DOG! IT DID HAPPEN!
SO YOU'RE NOT A PHANTOM.
CRACK
WOP
I'M A PRINCE!
HOW COULD YOU DO THAT TO THE PERSON WHO SAVED YOUR LIFE?
YOU OUTTA BE A LITTLE MORE GRATEFUL.
AND WATCH THE FACE. MY NOSE MIGHT FALL OFF.
SAVED MY LIFE?
THAT'S RIDICULOUS.
YOU'RE THE ONE WHO GOT HIT BY THE CAR!
DASHHH
KRRSHH
SHOOM
DI DON
DI DON
(AMBULANCE SIREN)
EH?
INSTANT REPLAY

THIS CAN'T BE ...
I FELT SORRY FOR YOU AND YOUR PATHETIC LIFE.
BUT... BUT... I...
I THREW MY LIFE AWAY FOR YOU?
HEY...JUST CHILL. YOU CAME BACK BEAUTIFUL, DIDN'T YOU?
BUT...I'M WARNING YOU, STAY AWAY FROM MY YUMIKO.
SOUNDS LIKE HE'S BEEN AROUND THE BLOCK A FEW TIMES.
...
BUT YOU'RE A DOG!
GRRR
GRRR
GRRRR
YOU KNOW WHO YOU'RE LOOKING FOR?
I'M LOOKING FOR THE GUY WHO TURNED ME INTO A DOG SO HE CAN TURN ME BACK INTO A HUMAN.
GRRRR

I KNOW HE'S AROUND HERE SOMEWHERE. I'VE BEEN SENSING HIS PRESENCE EVER SINCE YUMIKO STARTED COMING TO THIS SCHOOL.
HE'S DEFINITELY HERE.
AND HE'S IN THE GREEN-HOUSE.
...pfff...
WHAT A MUG.
SHOOM
I SENSED HE WAS AROUND THE DAY WE LEFT FOR AMERICA.
MY HAND! MY HAND! OUUUCH.
spurt
HEH.
THAT DAY YOU CAME TO OUR JUNIOR HIGH...
YUMIKO SAID THERE WAS A BOY WHO LOOKED JUST LIKE ME. I WANTED TO CHECK YOU OUT.
Heh heh.
BING
GRRR.
WHAT'S WRONG, MISTER?
I'M GETTING AN EVIL VIBE.

IS SOMEONE ELSE IN HERE?
GYAAAAAH
Eeeee!

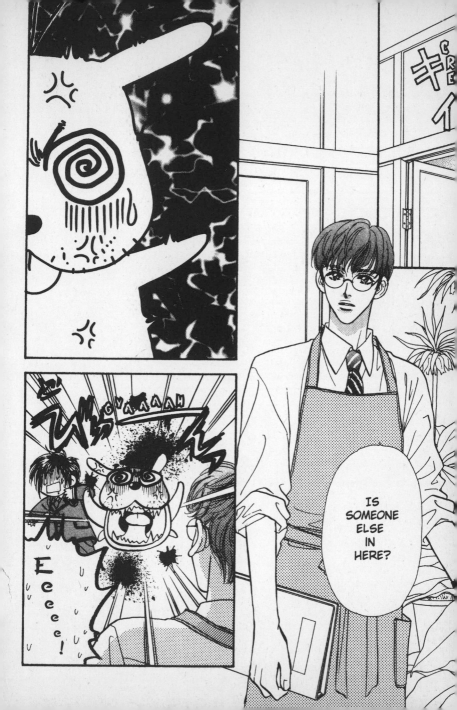

SHOOOM
whap
whap
whap
ARE YOU OKAY?
UHH... YAH.
HM?
MAN MADE?
HE CAN TELL!?

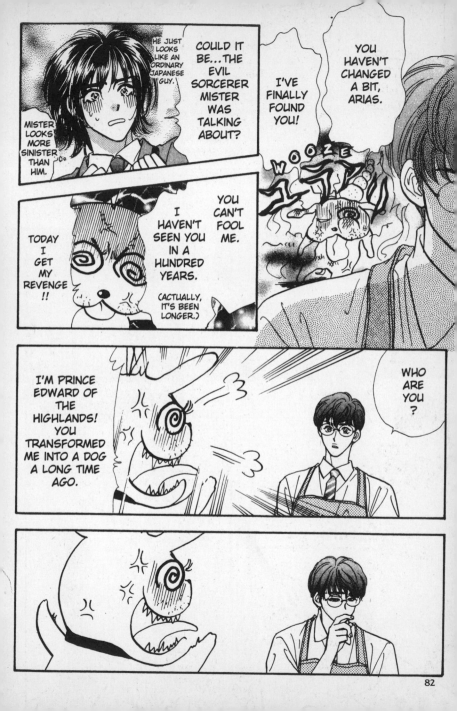

HE JUST LOOKS LIKE AN ORDINARY JAPANESE GUY.

MISTER LOOKS MORE SINISTER THAN HIM.

COULD IT BE...THE EVIL SORCERER MISTER WAS TALKING ABOUT?

I'VE FINALLY FOUND YOU!

YOU HAVEN'T CHANGED A BIT, ARIAS.

TODAY I GET MY REVENGE !!

I HAVEN'T SEEN YOU IN A HUNDRED YEARS.

YOU CAN'T FOOL ME.

(ACTUALLY, IT'S BEEN LONGER.)

I'M PRINCE EDWARD OF THE HIGHLANDS! YOU TRANSFORMED ME INTO A DOG A LONG TIME AGO.

WHO ARE YOU ?

AHHH!
ポーン!
TMP
EDWARD, THIRD IN LINE TO THE THRONE OF THAT PATHETIC, POVERTY-STRICKEN KINGDOM. YOU TRIED TO STEAL TWO PIGS FROM MY HUT, BUT ENDED UP ROLLING AROUND IN PIG POOP.
DIDN'T I TIE YOU TO A TREE OR SOMETHING?
Pi
ENOUGH WITH THE DETAILS!!
whoa.
あーははははは
hah hah hah hah
Aaah hah hah
ALL RIGHT ALREADY!!
IF YOU COMPLETELY FORGOT, THEN JUST CHANGE ME BACK AND BE DONE WITH IT!!
DO YOU HAVE ANY IDEA WHAT I'VE BEEN THROUGH!?
うわあああああ
UWAAAAAH
CAN'T.
えっ
HUH?
YOU'VE BEEN A DOG EVER SINCE!?

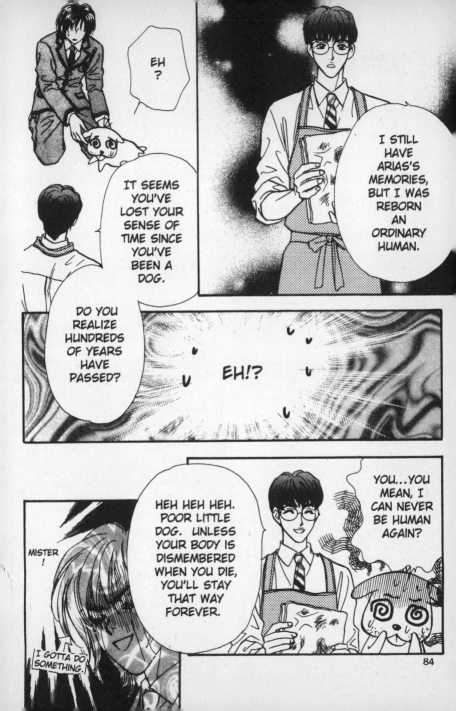

EH?

I STILL HAVE ARIAS'S MEMORIES, BUT I WAS REBORN AN ORDINARY HUMAN.

IT SEEMS YOU'VE LOST YOUR SENSE OF TIME SINCE YOU'VE BEEN A DOG.

DO YOU REALIZE HUNDREDS OF YEARS HAVE PASSED?

EH!?

HEH HEH HEH. POOR LITTLE DOG. UNLESS YOUR BODY IS DISMEMBERED WHEN YOU DIE, YOU'LL STAY THAT WAY FOREVER.

YOU...YOU MEAN, I CAN NEVER BE HUMAN AGAIN?

MISTER!

I GOTTA DO SOMETHING.

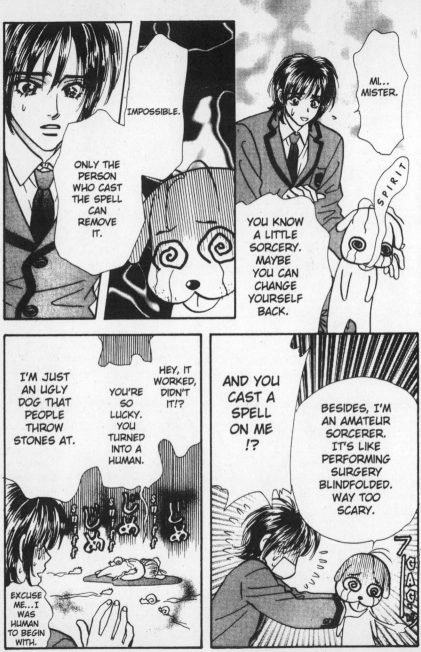

IMPOSSIBLE.

ONLY THE PERSON WHO CAST THE SPELL CAN REMOVE IT.

MI... MISTER.

SPIRIT

YOU KNOW A LITTLE SORCERY. MAYBE YOU CAN CHANGE YOURSELF BACK.

HEY, IT WORKED, DIDN'T IT!?

YOU'RE SO LUCKY. YOU TURNED INTO A HUMAN.

I'M JUST AN UGLY DOG THAT PEOPLE THROW STONES AT.

sniff sniff sniff sniff

EXCUSE ME...I WAS HUMAN TO BEGIN WITH.

AND YOU CAST A SPELL ON ME !?

BESIDES, I'M AN AMATEUR SORCERER. IT'S LIKE PERFORMING SURGERY BLINDFOLDED. WAY TOO SCARY.

GACK

CHEER UP, MISTER.
YOU HAVE YUMIKO.
AS FOR ME...
YUMIKO? ARE YOU TALKING ABOUT YUMIKO ITOH IN 2D?
ぎくっ
gulp
Grrrr...
YOU...YOU ...IF YOU LAY ONE FINGER ON MY YUMIKO...
I'M BACK! ♥
OH, HELLO PROFESSOR TAKAMURA.
あんあん
huff huff
...
HELLO MS. ITOH.

SORRY I TOOK SO LONG, MISTER.
HAVE YOU BEEN A GOOD BOY?
だだ
MISTER?
ぎゅう
HUG
...
MS. ITOH, MAY I SPEAK WITH YOU?
OKAY.
I THINK THIS CHERRY TREE IS READY TO TRANSPLANT OUTSIDE.
GRRR.

Gyaaah!
MIS-TER!?
CHOMP CHOMP
CHOMP
CHOMP
I'M SOOO SORRY PROFESSOR. ARE YOU ALL RIGHT!?
IT'S NOTHING.
DON'T WORRY.
YOU'D BETTER SEE THE NURSE RIGHT AWAY.
YANK
WHAT'S WRONG WITH YOU!? BAAAAD BOY!!
shake shake
NOW LET'S APOLOGIZE TO THE PROFESSOR!
I DON'T LIKE THIS KIND OF BEHAVIOR, YOU BAD BOY!
I HATE YOU!
YU... UH...
MS. ITOH.
UHH ... MISTER ...
OH, MS. ITOH...

WHAT DO YOU THINK ABOUT MEN WHO'VE HAD PLASTIC SURGERY?
HUH ?
PLASTIC SURGERY.
SNIFF SNIFF
I... I REALLY DON'T...

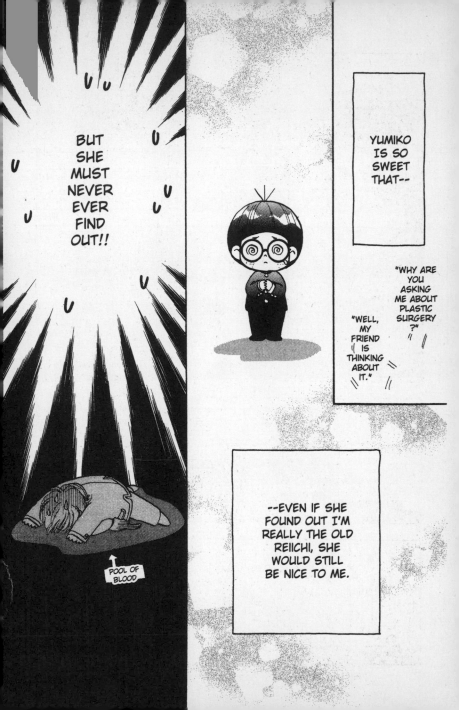

BUT SHE MUST NEVER EVER FIND OUT!!

POOL OF BLOOD

YUMIKO IS SO SWEET THAT--

"WELL, MY FRIEND IS THINKING ABOUT IT."

"WHY ARE YOU ASKING ME ABOUT PLASTIC SURGERY?"

--EVEN IF SHE FOUND OUT I'M REALLY THE OLD REIICHI, SHE WOULD STILL BE NICE TO ME.

WELCOME HOME.
HOW'D IT GO? HOW WAS YOUR HIGH SCHOOL DEBUT!?
DID YOU DO EVERYTHING THE WAY WE TRAINED YOU?
.....
じわっ glare
パタン BAM
THE JOOOOOY OF LOOOVE ALWAYS ENDS.
IT NEVER LAAAASTS.
IT NEVER LAAASTS FOR MEEEEE.

EHHH !?
YUMIKO !?
CAUTION: KEEP IT A SECRET.
WHOOOA.
WHAT A COINCIDENCE !
IT MUST BE FATE. GO FOR IT, REIICHI! ♡
B... BUT...
IT'S FINE. EVEN IF PLASTIC SURGERY TURNS HER OFF, AS LONG AS SHE DOESN'T KNOW, IT'S NOT A PROBLEM.
BESIDES YOU LOOK SO DIFFERENT !
I... I GUESS YOU'RE RIGHT.
REMEMBER WHAT I TAUGHT YOU? LOVE IS ABOUT PUTTING ON A GOOD PERFORMANCE.
TEE HEE.
IF YOU'RE CONSISTENT IN YOUR DECEPTION, EVEN A LIE BECOMES THE TRUTH.
I THINK YOU REALLY BELIEVE THAT.
WHAT DO YOU MEAN?
WACK

PROFESSOR TAKAMURA AND YUMIKO SEEM TO BE GETTING CLOSE.
MAN, I HAD MY EYE ON HIM.
I LIKE REIICHI SWAN. ♡
OH BROTHER, YOU USED TO SAY PROFESSOR TAKAMURA WAS YOUR WHOLE LIFE.
BUT REIICHI IS SOOOO CUTE.
TEE HEE HEE. ♡
カアアアア
BLUSH
GRRR GRRRR
イライライラ
イラ イラ
GRRRRR

THIS IS NO TIME TO BE SHY.
ARIAS IS FLIRTING WITH YUMIKO.
HE REALLY PISSES ME OFF!
IT'S OKAY. HE'S A TEACHER. THERE'S NOTHING TO WORRY ABOUT.
BOY, ARE YOU NAIVE.
THAT GUY HAS NO SCRUPLES.
IF HE GETS IN THE MOOD, HE'LL JUST GO FOR IT.
HE'S ALWAYS BEEN A PLAYER.
AHHH
HEY YOU. DON'T YOU HAVE THE GUTS TO ASK HER OUT?
EH!?
IF YUMIKO HAD A BOYFRIEND, SHE WOULDN'T BE HANGING OUT WITH THIS BOZO.
I'LL HELP YOU.
EHHH? BUT... BUT... I REALLY LIKE YUMIKO.
SNICKER
DON'T WORRY. YOU'RE NOT CAPABLE OF DOING ANYTHING LIKE THAT. ♡
JAB

I DON'T HAVE TO HAVE A RELATIONSHIP WITH HER.
I'M HAPPY JUST BEING NEAR HER.
WHY AM I SO SHY?
IF YOU'RE SO WORRIED, WHY DON'T YOU TELL YUMIKO?
YOU TELL ME EVERYTHING. SHE'S YOUR OWNER. WHY DO YOU KEEP SECRETS FROM HER?
IF SHE FINDS OUT I'M NOT A DOG, IT'S GONNA BE A BIG MESS.
pffff.
A BIG MESS ?
MISTER LOOKS SO FLUFFY TODAY.
HE'S SO HUGGABLE.
YEAH. WE TOOK A BATH TOGETHER LAST NIGHT. ♡

YOU REALLY SHOULDN'T BE BATHING WITH HIM.
WHAT IF HE'S REALLY A HUMAN THAT WAS TURNED INTO A DOG BY A SORCERER ?
WHY NOT ?
THAT WOULD BE SOOO COOL.
IF HE WERE HUMAN, I'D MARRY HIM.
BGUUUSH
ぽわーん
I'M SURE MISTER WOULD MAKE AN AMAZING HUMAN! ♡
MS. ITOH, HOW MANY FINGERS DO YOU SEE?
THREE.
SHE GOT IT.
WELL, I HAPPEN TO HAVE TWO TICKETS TO THE ROSE EXHIBITION ON SATURDAY. WOULD YOU LIKE TO GO?
DIDN'T YOU SAY YOU WANTED TO GROW ROSES?

I HAVE TO TAKE MISTER IN FOR HIS SHOTS ON SATURDAY.
大前さん
先生が
MS. OMAE, PROFESSOR TAKAMURA HAS...
MS. OMAE SAID SHE WANTED TO SEE THAT SHOW.
NEVER-MIND.
YUMIKO'S KIND OF STRANGE, ISN'T SHE?
SHE SURE IS.
IF I WERE HER, I'D GO TO THE EXHIBITION AND GET SHOTS FOR THE DOG ANOTHER TIME.
...
MS. MURASE, DO YOU LIKE ROSES?
GRIN
I DO! ♡

I'M GOING.
SEE YOU TOMORROW.
CAN YOU LOCK UP THE GREEN-HOUSE, REIICHI?
SURE THING.
snort snort
YUMIKO'S STILL NOT BACK.
I WONDER IF SHE'S IN THE GREEN-HOUSE.
YUMIKO?

YU...
SHE'S SLEEP-ING?
IT'S SO WARM IN HERE.
すぴzzzz
th-thump
どき。

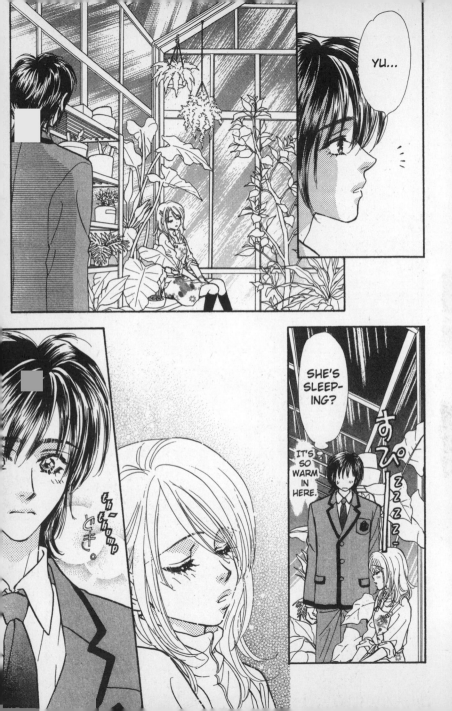

BUT IT'S NO USE.
I MAY LOOK DIFFERENT, BUT INSIDE I'M STILL THE SAME OLD HELMET.
I'M NOT A GOOD MATCH FOR YUMIKO.
WHAT I TOLD MISTER ISN'T TRUE.
I REALLY DO WANT TO BE MORE THAN JUST FRIENDS.

MAYBE.
どき th-thump
どき th-thump
BUT --
どき th-thump
--ON THE SURFACE I AM A GOOD MATCH FOR HER.
どき th-thump
MAYBE JUST A LITTLE.
どき th-thump
どき th-thump
ZZZ
スカッ

HUH
?

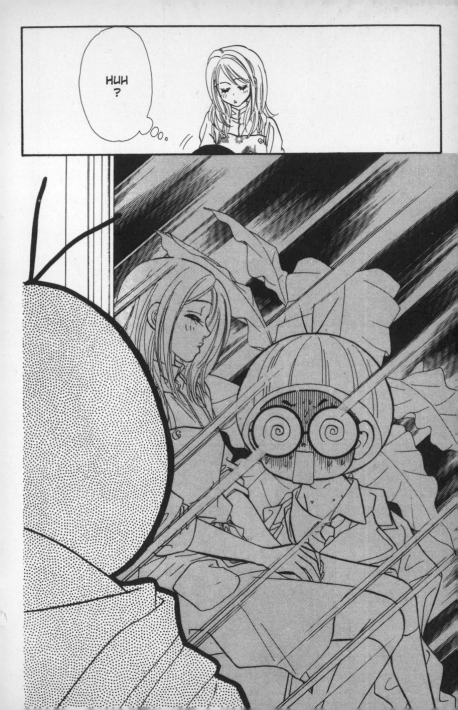

WHOA.
I CHANGED BACK !?
WHAT !?
EEEE
HOW DID THIS HAPPEN !!? MISTER, HELP!!!
EE
NNN.

HMM.
I MUST'VE FALLEN ASLEEP.
AAaaahhh.
THAT FELT GOOD.
WHOA. IT'S PITCH DARK OUT.
キョロ
WHHIP
I BET EVERYONE'S GONE.
DID SOME-ONE DROP THESE?
PEOPLE SHOULDN'T BE SO CARELESS WITH THE KEYS.
カサッ
RUSTLE
HUH?
IS SOMEONE IN HERE?
REMEMBER WHAT YOUR SISTERS TOLD YOU.

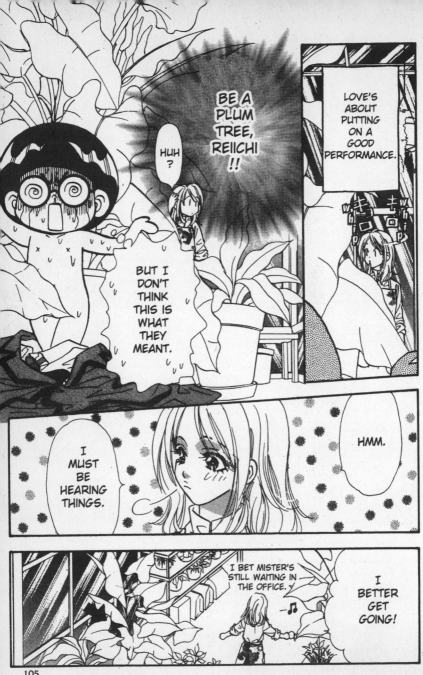

LOVE'S ABOUT PUTTING ON A GOOD PERFORMANCE.

BE A PLUM TREE, REIICHI!!

HUH?

BUT I DON'T THINK THIS IS WHAT THEY MEANT.

I MUST BE HEARING THINGS.

HMM.

I BET MISTER'S STILL WAITING IN THE OFFICE.

I BETTER GET GOING!

CLICK
バタン
Bang
ホッ
click
ガチャ
K-CHK
ガチャ
K-CHK
ガチャー!
K-CHK
UH-OH.
ALL LOCKED UP?
REIICHI STILL ISN'T HOME.
HE DID IT. HE'S SPENDING THE NIGHT WITH HER!
HE'S FINALLY A MAN!
YAY! I'LL MAKE A CAKE TO CELEBRATE.

★ EPISODE 1 ★ THE END

EPISODE
2

チュー!
CHEEP
チュー!
CHEEP
ピチチチ…
tweeeet
TRAAA LA.
LA LA LA. ♪
ガチャ
jiggle
ガチャ
jiggle
TRA LA LA. ♬
ガチャ
GOOD MORNING, EVERYONE. ♡
HOW ARE ALL OF YOU THIS MORNING?
LA LA LA.
♪
カサ
rustle…

MY GORGEOUS MARGURITES! WHAT'S THAT?
DID YOU SAY I'M THE GORGEOUS ONE? OH, YOU ♡ SILLY FLOWERS!
TIP TOE
RATTLE!
TOK TOK TOK TOK TOK
...PEE.
?
TURNING YELLOW
GOTTA PEE !!

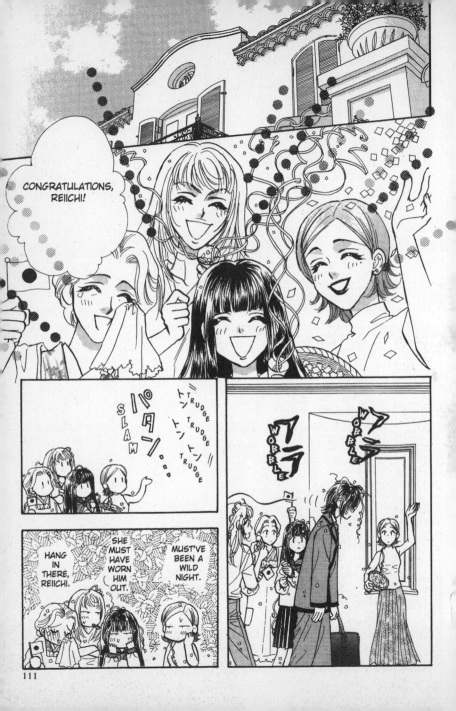

CONGRATULATIONS, REIICHI!

SLAM

TRUDGE
TRUDGE
TRUDGE

WOBBLE

WOBBLE

HANG IN THERE, REIICHI.

SHE MUST HAVE WORN HIM OUT.

MUST'VE BEEN A WILD NIGHT.

GOOD THING I GOT MY GOOD LOOKS BACK.
FWOP
BUT HOW DID THAT HAPPEN?
I'VE BEEN FINE FOR MONTHS.
DID THE SPELL WEAR OFF LIKE IN CINDERELLA?
OR WAS IT BECAUSE I TRIED TO TAKE ADVANTAGE OF YUMIKO WHILE SHE WAS ASLEEP?

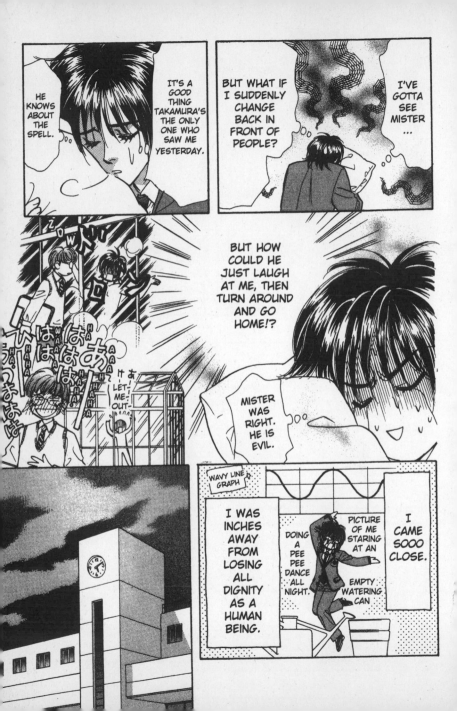

HE KNOWS ABOUT THE SPELL.

IT'S A GOOD THING TAKAMURA'S THE ONLY ONE WHO SAW ME YESTERDAY.

BUT WHAT IF I SUDDENLY CHANGE BACK IN FRONT OF PEOPLE?

I'VE GOTTA SEE MISTER...

BUT HOW COULD HE JUST LAUGH AT ME, THEN TURN AROUND AND GO HOME!?

HA HA WAAA HAHA AAA HA IT! AH LET ME OUT

MISTER WAS RIGHT. HE IS EVIL.

WAVY LINE GRAPH

I WAS INCHES AWAY FROM LOSING ALL DIGNITY AS A HUMAN BEING.

DOING A PEE PEE DANCE ALL NIGHT.

PICTURE OF ME STARING AT AN EMPTY WATERING CAN

I CAME SOOO CLOSE.

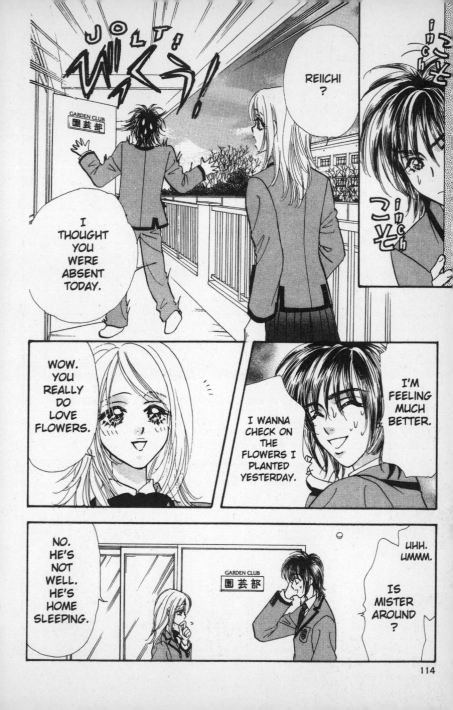

REIICHI?

I THOUGHT YOU WERE ABSENT TODAY.

WOW. YOU REALLY DO LOVE FLOWERS.

I WANNA CHECK ON THE FLOWERS I PLANTED YESTERDAY.

I'M FEELING MUCH BETTER.

NO. HE'S NOT WELL. HE'S HOME SLEEPING.

UHH. UMMM.

IS MISTER AROUND?

GARDEN CLUB
園芸部

WHAAAT!?
MISTER'S NOT COMING TODAY?
HE'S GOT A SLIGHT COLD. THAT'S ALL. NOTHING TO WORRY ABOUT.
WHAT AM I GONNA DO?
I COULD CHANGE BACK ANY MINUTE. I GOTTA SEE MISTER RIGHT AWAY!
IS IT...
IS IT OKAY IF I GO CHECK ON HIM?
UHHH. SURE.
THANK GOD!
FOR NOW.
ホッ
WHEW
...
WAIT HERE WHILE I GET MY STUFF.
GARDEN C
園芸
HUH?

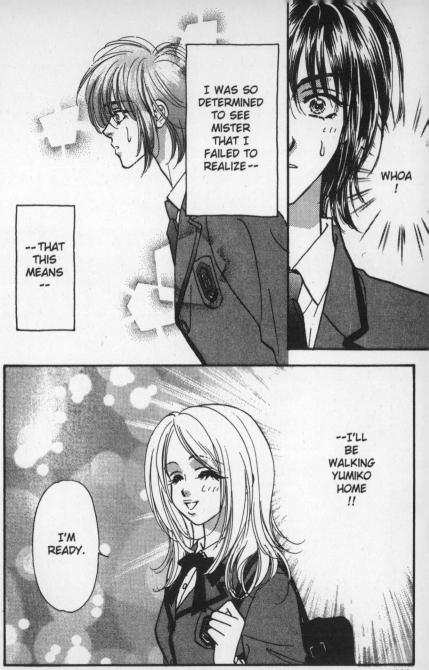

I WAS SO DETERMINED TO SEE MISTER THAT I FAILED TO REALIZE--

--THAT THIS MEANS--

WHOA!

--I'LL BE WALKING YUMIKO HOME!!

I'M READY.

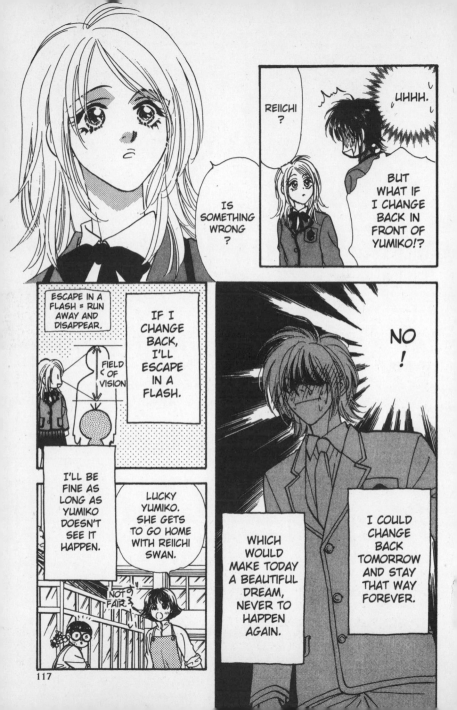

REIICHI?

UHHH.

IS SOMETHING WRONG?

BUT WHAT IF I CHANGE BACK IN FRONT OF YUMIKO!?

ESCAPE IN A FLASH = RUN AWAY AND DISAPPEAR.

FIELD OF VISION

IF I CHANGE BACK, I'LL ESCAPE IN A FLASH.

NO!

I'LL BE FINE AS LONG AS YUMIKO DOESN'T SEE IT HAPPEN.

LUCKY YUMIKO. SHE GETS TO GO HOME WITH REIICHI SWAN.

NOT FAIR.

WHICH WOULD MAKE TODAY A BEAUTIFUL DREAM, NEVER TO HAPPEN AGAIN.

I COULD CHANGE BACK TOMORROW AND STAY THAT WAY FOREVER.

REIICHI, WILL YOU WALK ME HOME TOMORROW ♡ ?
BYE. SEE YA.
...
THE OLD ME ...
WOULD'VE BEEN TOO ASHAMED TO WALK HER HOME.
YUMIKO --
BUT NOW EVERYTHING IS DIFFERENT. EVERYONE LIKES ME.
HUH ?
--MAY I CARRY YOUR BAG?
I'M GLAD I'M BEAUTIFUL, EVEN IF IT WAS A HAPHAZARD SPELL.
REIICHI.
THANK YOU.
HUH ?
FOR CARRYING YOUR BAG?

I THINK MISTER IS THE CUTEST DOG IN THE WORLD, BUT NO ONE ELSE THINKS SO.
NOT ONLY FOR CARRYING MY BAG.
...
SEEING YOU SO WORRIED ABOUT HIM MAKES ME REALIZE YOU CARE ABOUT HIM AS MUCH AS I DO.
GULP
WAIT. THERE'S ONE OTHER PERSON. THE OTHER REIICHI SWAN.
HE'S THE ONE WHO FOUND MISTER WHEN HE WAS LOST.
TEE HEE.
THAT'S WHY I'M SO GRATEFUL.

MISTER'S GONNA BE SO HAPPY TO SEE YOU.
YUMIKO.
どきん TH-THUMP
TH-THUMP どきん
どきん TH-THUMP
BRUSH

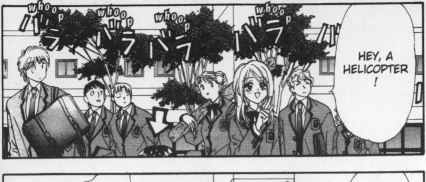

HEY, A HELICOPTER!

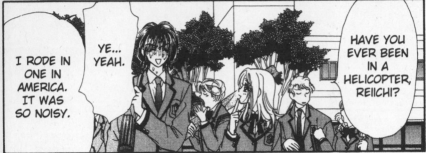

HAVE YOU EVER BEEN IN A HELICOPTER, REIICHI?

YE... YEAH.

I RODE IN ONE IN AMERICA. IT WAS SO NOISY.

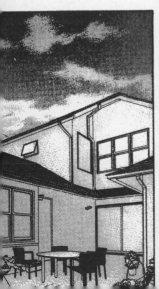

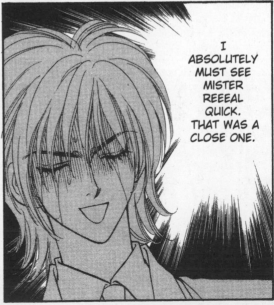

I ABSOLUTELY MUST SEE MISTER REEEAL QUICK. THAT WAS A CLOSE ONE.

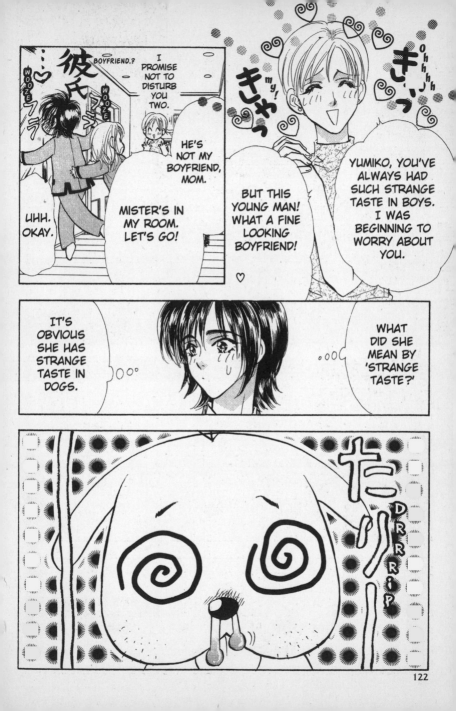

BOYFRIEND.?

I PROMISE NOT TO DISTURB YOU TWO.

HE'S NOT MY BOYFRIEND, MOM.

MISTER'S IN MY ROOM. LET'S GO!

UHH. OKAY.

BUT THIS YOUNG MAN! WHAT A FINE LOOKING BOYFRIEND!

YUMIKO, YOU'VE ALWAYS HAD SUCH STRANGE TASTE IN BOYS. I WAS BEGINNING TO WORRY ABOUT YOU.

IT'S OBVIOUS SHE HAS STRANGE TASTE IN DOGS.

WHAT DID SHE MEAN BY 'STRANGE TASTE?'

DRRRIP

WHAT A MUG.
WHOOOA.
HOW ARE YOU FEELING, MISTER?
ACHOO
REIICHI CAME TO SEE YOU.
NOW STAY STILL.
ALL THIS TIME --
--I'VE BEEN THINKING ABOUT MY OWN PROBLEMS, AND HERE MISTER IS A HUMAN WHO CAN NEVER CHANGE BACK.
IT MUST BE MISERABLE FOR HIM.
HE'S IN MUCH WORSE SHAPE THAN I AM.
sniff

HE LOOKS SO WEAK.
POOR MISTER.
YOUR HAIR IS SO COARSE IT TAKES FOREVER TO DRY.
I TOLD YOU YOU'D CATCH A COLD IF YOU TOOK A BATH EVERYDAY.
I'M NOT LETTING YOU IN THE BATHTUB ANYMORE.
YU...
YUMIKO.
MISTER LOVES TAKING BATHS. HE ALWAYS FOLLOWS ME IN.
GULP
DO YOU TAKE BATHS WITH MISTER?
YUMIKO, YOUR TEA IS READY!
COMING.
...
I'LL BE RIGHT BACK.

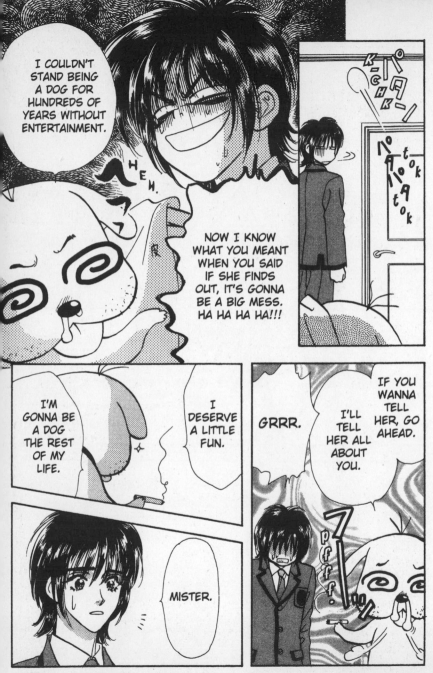

I COULDN'T STAND BEING A DOG FOR HUNDREDS OF YEARS WITHOUT ENTERTAINMENT.

HEH.

NOW I KNOW WHAT YOU MEANT WHEN YOU SAID IF SHE FINDS OUT, IT'S GONNA BE A BIG MESS. HA HA HA HA!!!

K-CHA-K-!

po tok po tok

I'M GONNA BE A DOG THE REST OF MY LIFE.

I DESERVE A LITTLE FUN.

MISTER.

GRRR.

I'LL TELL HER ALL ABOUT YOU.

IF YOU WANNA TELL HER, GO AHEAD.

pfff.

HMMMM
IF I KEEP MY COOL AND LOOK AT IT REALISTICALLY --
--I REALIZE IT WOULD BE TOUGH FOR ME TO SUDDENLY CHANGE BACK INTO A HUMAN BEING. JAPAN ISN'T WHAT IT WAS A HUNDRED YEARS AGO.
I'VE GOT NO MONEY, NO REFERENCES AND I'M NOT REGISTERED WITH THE CENSUS.
...
I'M ACCUSTOMED TO BEING TAKEN CARE OF. I CAN'T IMAGINE HAVING TO WORK.
FACT IS, I'M A PRINCE. I'M JUST NOT THE WORKING CLASS TYPE.
WHAT A DOG.
WHAT ABOUT PROFESSOR TAKAMURA? YOU WERE SO MAD AT HIM.
REMEMBER ?
YOU SAID HE'D GO FOR IT IF HE GOT THE CHANCE.
DON'T YOU CARE IF HE TAKES ADVANTAGE OF YUMIKO ?
AS A DOG YOU'VE GOT NO CHANCE AGAINST HIM.
I WON'T LET HIM!! YUMIKO IS MINE!!!

AHHH. WOULDN'T IT BE GREAT IF I COULD BE A HUMAN BEING WHENEVER I FELT LIKE IT AND A DOG THE REST OF THE TIME?
GRRR.
IF I WERE A HUMAN, I'D NEVER BE ABLE TO WATCH YUMIKO BECOME A WOMAN.
THERE ARE ADVANTAGES TO BEING A DOG.
Yank!
TWAAAA~
OUCH! WHAT DO YOU THINK YOU'RE DOING?
YOU CAST THAT TWO-BIT SPELL ON ME AND I KEEP CHANGING BACK WHEN I DON'T WANT TO!
I WAS A FOOL FOR FEELING SORRY FOR YOU!
NNGGG
HEEEY.
I TOLD YOU MY SORCERY WASN'T ALL THAT GOOD.
AHH, SO I BLEW IT?
WHEN DID YOU CHANGE BACK?
UHH.

WH... WH... WHEN I WAS ABOUT TO KISS HER ON THE CHEEK AND WHEN I TRIED TO HOLD HER HAND.
YUMIKO'S.
S
SPEW
NOT IN A MILLION YEARS.
WHAT MAKES YOU THINK YOU CAN BE SO BOLD JUST BECAUSE YOU'RE GOOD LOOKING? YOU'RE STILL HELMET INSIDE.
WHEW. THAT FELT GOOD.
DIDN'T YOU SAY YOU WERE HAPPY JUST TO BE NEAR HER?
GLOP
I CAN'T BREATHE.
GLOP
THAT NEARLY KILLED ME.
I COULDN'T HELP IT. I'M A GUY!
GUESS I DON'T HAVE TO WORRY ABOUT YOU. IF YOU MAKE A MOVE ON HER, YOU GO BACK TO YOUR OLD UGLY SELF.
GRRR.
HEH HEH
TSK TSK
AND I CAN'T 'CAUSE I'M A DOG.
REMEMBER, IF YOU TOUCH HER, YOU GET WHAT YOU DESERVE. MY SORCERY WAS PERFECT!

WELL.
YOU DESERVE TO BE A DOG!
YOU TRIED TO MAKE ME THINK THE PROFESSOR WAS EVIL, BUT I'D SAY IT'S THE OTHER WAY AROUND.
OF THE TWO OF YOU, YOU'RE MUCH MUCH WORSE.
WHAT THE ...
きゃあ
EEEK
きゃあ
EEEEEK
NEVER MIND. I CAME HERE TO SEE IF YOU COULD HELP ME, BUT I DON'T TRUST YOU.
I'M BETTER OFF TALKING TO PROFESSOR TAKAMURA.
ムカッ
HMPH.
THE TRUTH HURTS, DOESN'T IT?
HAH HA!!
WHY WOULD I HELP YOU HIT ON YUMIKO?

HIK-CHK
SORRY THAT TOOK SO LONG. ♡
pant pant
I'LL BE GOING NOW.
HUH? SO SOON?
I THINK MISTER NEEDS TO REST.
MISTER, REIICHI IS LEAVING.
HEY, WHAT'S WRONG?
MISTER?

THIS SAFFRON.
WOW! YOU CAN TELL IT'S SAFFRON?
JUST FROM THE LEAVES ?
I GOT THAT FROM THE OTHER REIICHI SWAN IN JUNIOR HIGH.
I DIVIDED AND TRANSPLANTED IT. I'M HOPING TO GET MORE PLANTS.

YUMIKO.
YOU MUST ... TREASURE IT.
HUH?
UHHH. I MEAN YOU'RE DOING A GOOD JOB.
TEE HEE HEE.

WHAT AM I GONNA DO?
I LIKE YUMIKO NOW MORE THAN EVER.
I LIKE HER SOOO MUCH. I REALLY DON'T KNOW WHAT TO DO.
I KEEP TELLING MYSELF I JUST WANT TO BE HER FRIEND, BUT--

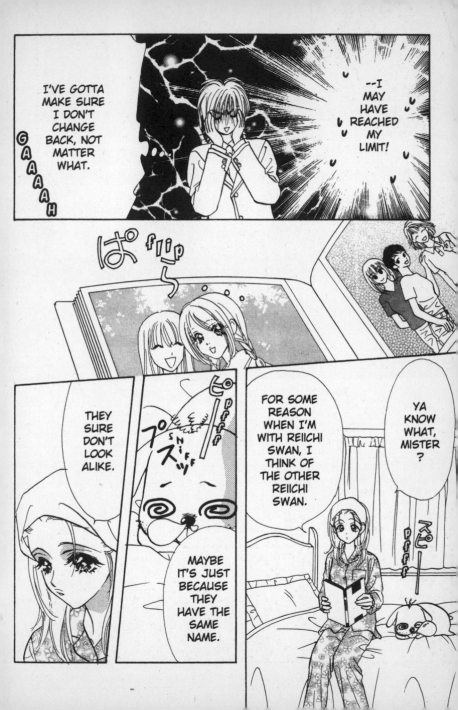

GAAAAH

I'VE GOTTA MAKE SURE I DON'T CHANGE BACK, NOT MATTER WHAT.

--I MAY HAVE REACHED MY LIMIT!

ぱ flip ら

THEY SURE DON'T LOOK ALIKE.

SNIFF

MAYBE IT'S JUST BECAUSE THEY HAVE THE SAME NAME.

FOR SOME REASON WHEN I'M WITH REIICHI SWAN, I THINK OF THE OTHER REIICHI SWAN.

YA KNOW WHAT, MISTER?

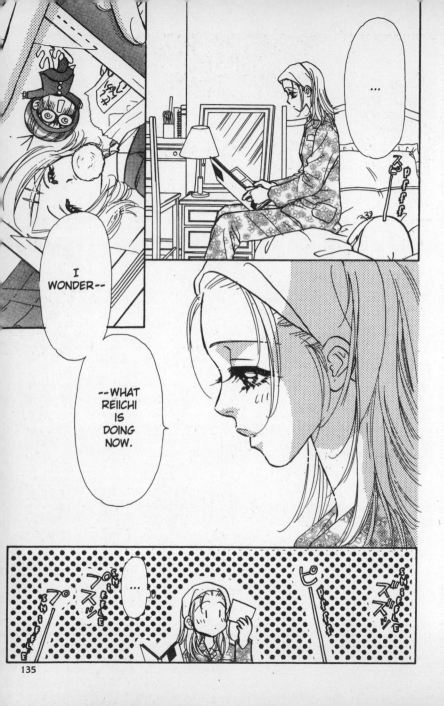

I WONDER--

--WHAT REIICHI IS DOING NOW.

...

135

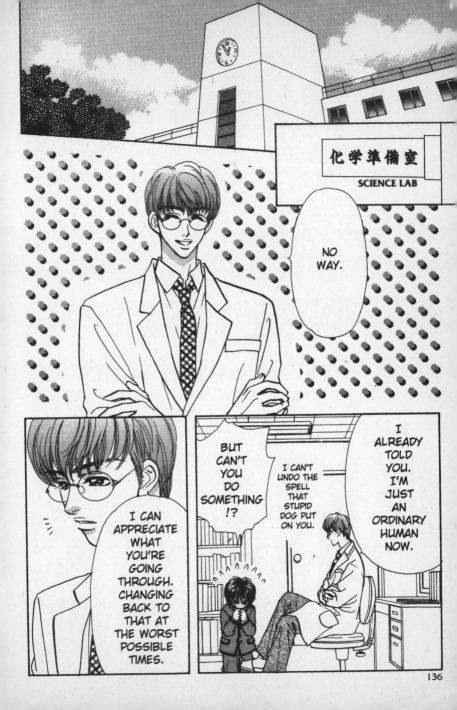

化学準備室
SCIENCE LAB

NO WAY.

I CAN APPRECIATE WHAT YOU'RE GOING THROUGH. CHANGING BACK TO THAT AT THE WORST POSSIBLE TIMES.

BUT CAN'T YOU DO SOMETHING!?

I CAN'T UNDO THE SPELL THAT STUPID DOG PUT ON YOU.

I ALREADY TOLD YOU. I'M JUST AN ORDINARY HUMAN NOW.

...
...
Phew
YUMIKO ITOH, HUH?
SHE'S NOT MY USUAL TYPE, BUT SHE INTRIGUES ME.
PROFESSOR?
chuckle chuckle
WHEN SHE DIDN'T RESPOND TO MY ADVANCES, IT MADE ME WANT HER EVEN MORE.
IT'S NO USE.
MISTER WAS NO HELP, SO I WAS TOTALLY COUNTING ON TAKAMURA.
WHAT A MISTAKE!
PROFESSOR, YOU'RE ALL I'VE GOT!
?
CLASP
PLEEEASE HELP ME!!

...
I WAS JUST GIVING YOU A ROUGH TIME.
I CAN'T USE SORCERY, BUT I'LL SEE WHAT I CAN DO.
IT'S HOPE-LESS.
I'LL TRY MY BEST.
THAAAANK YOU.
SO, YOU ONLY CHANGE BACK WHEN YOU'RE NEAR YUMIKO?
UHHH.
I THINK SO.
WELL, LET'S TRY HER.
GO!
EHHH?

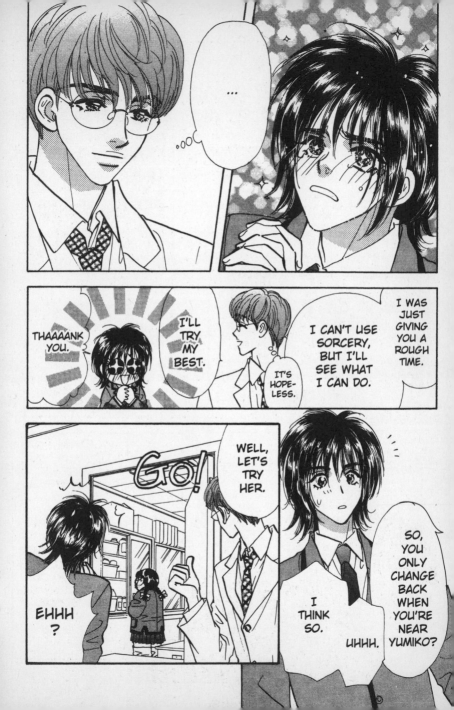

NO WAY!
I CAN'T!!
IT'S JUST AN EXPERIMENT.
BESIDES, SHE'S GOT BIG BREASTS.
N... NOO-OO!
I CAN'T DO IT!
THIS IS NO TIME TO BE FUSSY.
NOW'S YOUR CHANCE. SHE'S ALONE.
I'LL COVER FOR YOU IN CASE YOU CHANGE BACK.
IT'S FINE. TRY TO IMAGINE THAT YOUR LIFE DEPENDS ON IT.
BU... BU... BUT.
IT'S ESSENTIAL FOR ME TO KNOW. OTHERWISE I CAN'T HELP YOU.
gulp
UHH.
MS. OMAE.

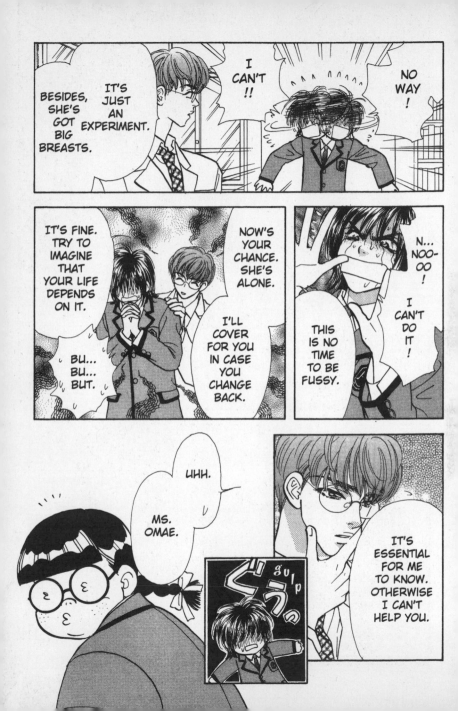

LOOKS LIKE YOU'RE WORKING ON AN EXPERIMENT.
MR. SWAN ?
CAN I HELP ?
TH... THANKS.
...
rattle
rattle
NOW ...
HOW AM I GONNA DO THIS?
SHHK

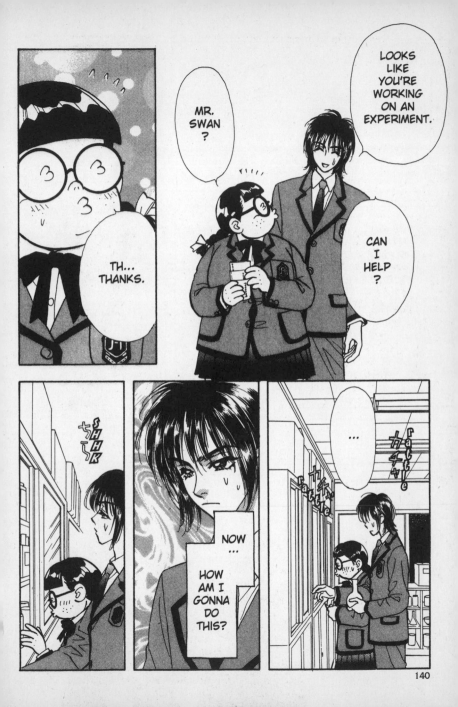

I'LL JUST ...
I'LL JUST GRAB HER HAND.
じーっ
STARE
REI..
REI-ICHI?
じり
CRINGE
じり
CRINGE
どきん
th-thump
どきん
th-thump
どきん
th-thump
どきん
th-thump
どきん
th-thump
どきん
th-thump
ぴくっ

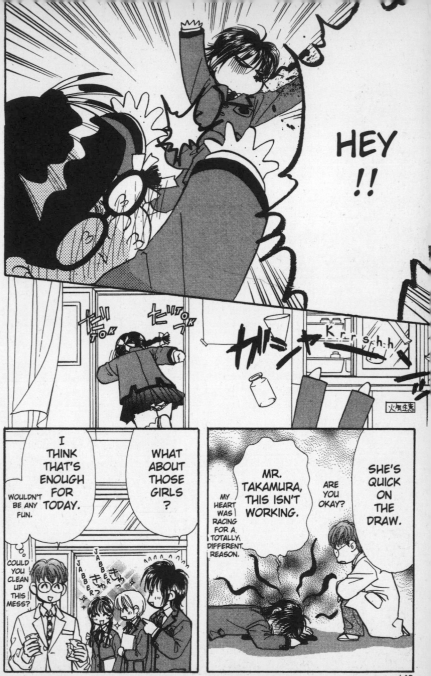

HEY
!!

I THINK THAT'S ENOUGH FOR TODAY.

WHAT ABOUT THOSE GIRLS?

WOULDN'T BE ANY FUN.

COULD YOU CLEAN UP THIS MESS?

MR. TAKAMURA, THIS ISN'T WORKING.

MY HEART WAS RACING FOR A TOTALLY DIFFERENT REASON.

ARE YOU OKAY?

SHE'S QUICK ON THE DRAW.

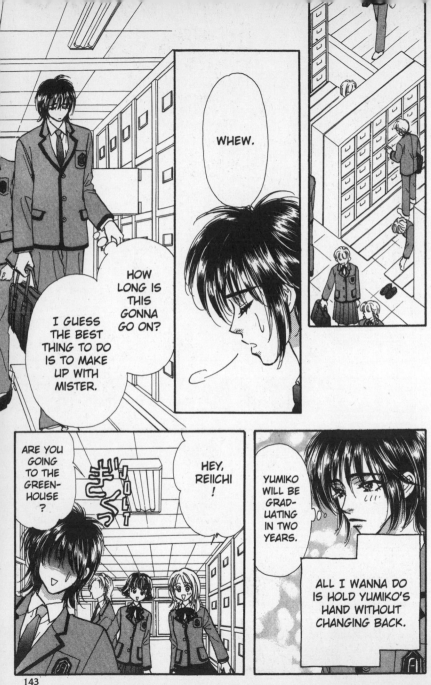

WHEW.

HOW LONG IS THIS GONNA GO ON?

I GUESS THE BEST THING TO DO IS TO MAKE UP WITH MISTER.

ARE YOU GOING TO THE GREEN-HOUSE?

HEY, REIICHI!

YUMIKO WILL BE GRADUATING IN TWO YEARS.

ALL I WANNA DO IS HOLD YUMIKO'S HAND WITHOUT CHANGING BACK.

THANKS SO MUCH FOR COMING OVER YESTERDAY. ♡
MY MOM WANTS YOU TO COME OVER AGAIN.
THANKS.
SO...
HOW'S MISTER?
NOT SO GOOD.
HE HAS NO APPETITE AND NO ENERGY.
REALLY?
HE WAS BEING A JERK, BUT MAYBE HE ACTUALLY ISN'T WELL.
MAYBE HE IS SICK.
きゅうん
whimper
I SHOULDN'T HAVE BEEN SO ROUGH WITH HIM.

I'M SORRY, MISTER.
EEEE.
WOW!! LOVE LETTERS! TWO OF THEM!
WHO ARE THEY FROM!?
JOLT
HMM.
YOU'RE SOOO POPULAR, YUMIKO.
HOW MANY HAVE YOU GOTTEN SO FAR?
HUH? NOT THAT MANY.
...
I'M SCREWED.
I GOTTA STOP THINKING I'VE GOT TWO YEARS TO WIN YUMIKO OVER.

YUMIKO IS SO PRETTY. SHE'S BOUND TO GET A BOYFRIEND SOON.
WHAT SHOULD I DO?
IF YOU DON'T WANNA REJECT THEM, WHY DON'T YOU JUST GO OUT WITH THEM.
DO YOU LIKE ANYONE SPECIAL, YUMIKO?
ANYONE SPECIAL.
ITOH 伊藤
th-thump ドキッ

AH HAHHH! YOU DO!!
HUH? I DON'T REALLY KNOW.
EH?
WHAT DO YOU MEAN?
I'M NOT GOOD AT STUFF LIKE THAT.
I DON'T KNOW WHAT IT MEANS TO LIKE SOMEONE.
HMPH.
I GOTTA GO.
I'VE GOTTA STUDY-CRAM SESSION.
COULD YOU WATER MY FLOWERS?
SURE. SEE YOU LATER.
WHAT SHOULD I DO?

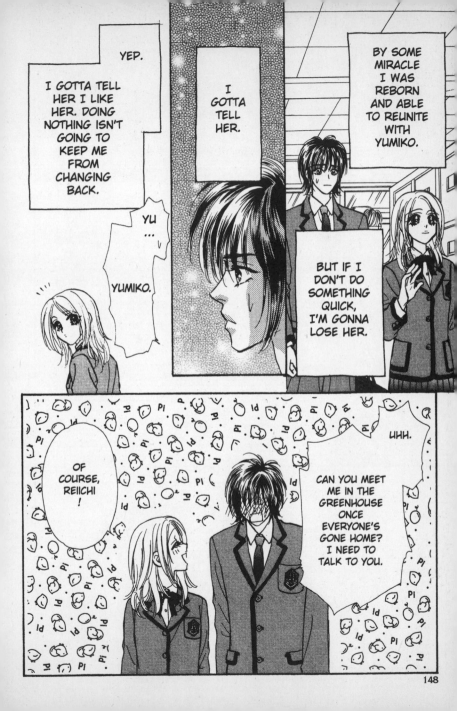

YEP.

I GOTTA TELL HER I LIKE HER. DOING NOTHING ISN'T GOING TO KEEP ME FROM CHANGING BACK.

I GOTTA TELL HER.

BY SOME MIRACLE I WAS REBORN AND ABLE TO REUNITE WITH YUMIKO.

YU...

YUMIKO.

BUT IF I DON'T DO SOMETHING QUICK, I'M GONNA LOSE HER.

OF COURSE, REIICHI!

UHH.

CAN YOU MEET ME IN THE GREENHOUSE ONCE EVERYONE'S GONE HOME? I NEED TO TALK TO YOU.

148

SEE YA.
THANKS, PROFESSOR TAKAMURA.
SEE YOU GUYS TOMORROW.
パターン
K-CHK
きゃっ
jabber
きゃっ
jabber
カタン
SCREEE

YUMIKO ITO. BORN MARCH 24. ARIES. BLOOD-TYPE O.
4/8 MISTER BIT MR. TAKAMURA.
4/10 I GAVE MISTER A BATH.
4/11 MISTER GOT SICK. I PLANTED PRIMROSES.
SHE'S EITHER AT THE GREEN-HOUSE OR TAKING CARE OF HER DOG ON WEEK-ENDS.
DOESN'T LOOK LIKE SHE HAS A BOYFRIEND.
ぱら flip
SO THE REASON SHE'S NOT RESPONDING TO ME ISN'T BECAUSE SHE HAS A BOYFRIEND.
ぱら flip
HMMM.
ぱら flip

しか
せんべい
CRACKERS FOR DEER
...
K-CHK
PROFESSOR TAKAMURA ?
YOU'RE STILL HERE ?

GOOD WORK, MS. ITOH.
I CAN LOCK UP TONIGHT.
ALL RIGHT.
GOOD NIGHT, PROFESSOR.
GOOD NIGHT.
OH... MS. ITOH ?
REMEMBER WHEN YOU SAID YOU WOULDN'T LIKE A GUY WHO'D HAD PLASTIC SURGERY?
... UHHH.
COULD YOU TELL ME WHY ?
EH? DID I SAY THAT?
HMMM.

I GUESS I'M NOT REALLY ATTRACTED TO HANDSOME FACES.
PLASTIC SURGERY SEEMS LIKE A WASTE.
A PERSON'S ORIGINAL FACE IS MORE REAL.
th-thump
th-thump
th-thump
th-thump
th-thump
th-thump

UHHH.
th-thump th-thump th-thump th-thump
th-thump th-thump th-thump th-thump
CALM DOWN! JUST CALM DOWN, REIICHI!
I'M FINE NOW. I'M NOT THAT UGLY HELMET ANY MORE.
WHHP WHHP
I WONDER IF SHE'LL COME.
SHE'S COMING.
I DON'T WANT TO REGRET ANYTHING, SO I HAVE TO TELL YUMIKO.
K-CHK—!

YUMI ...
REI ...
REIICHI.

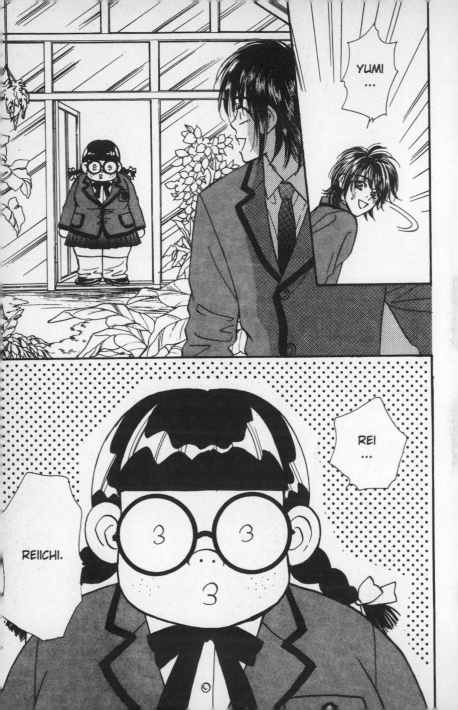

UHHH ... MS. OMAE.
HUH ?
I'M SORRY ABOUT HOW I REACTED TODAY.
IT HAPPENED SO SUDDENLY. I JUST WASN'T READY.
I MUST ADMIT, YOU KINDA SCARED ME.
BUT, I'M OKAY NOW.
teehee
I'M READY NOW.
READY FOR ANYTHING.
UHH... UHHH.
I WON'T RUN AWAY THIS TIME.
Blush

JAB
I LIKE YOU!
I LIKE YOU!
UGH.
I LIKE YOU!
AAH.
I LIKE YOU!
JAB
JAB
JAB
JAB
JAB

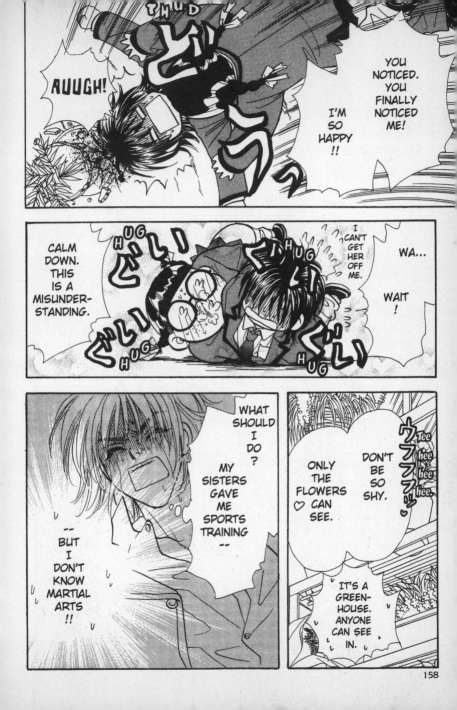

AUUGH!

I'M SO HAPPY!!

YOU NOTICED. YOU FINALLY NOTICED ME!

CALM DOWN. THIS IS A MISUNDERSTANDING.

I CAN'T GET HER OFF ME.

WA...

WAIT!

WHAT SHOULD I DO?

MY SISTERS GAVE ME SPORTS TRAINING --

-- BUT I DON'T KNOW MARTIAL ARTS!!

ONLY THE FLOWERS ♡ CAN SEE.

DON'T BE SO SHY.

IT'S A GREENHOUSE. ANYONE CAN SEE IN.

I NEVER GOT INTO A JAM LIKE THIS WHEN I WAS UGLY.
IT'S BEEN NOTHING BUT TROUBLE SINCE I'VE BEEN GOOD LOOKING.
YUMIKO, I CAN'T STAND IT ANYMORE.
I HAVE TO TELL YOU HOW I FEEL AT LEAST ONCE BEFORE I DIE.
GOD.
I CAN'T STAND IT ANYMORE.
I'M SEEING VISIONS OF YOU.

UHHHH.
YOU WANTED TO TALK TO ME.
YUMIKO.

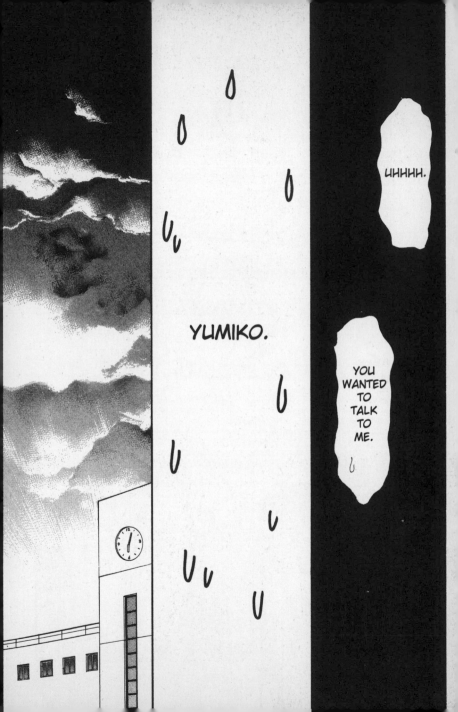

CAAAAW
CAAAW
I'M SO SORRY. THIS IS A BAD TIME.
WE CAN TALK LATER.
sniff
TRUDGE
TRUDGE

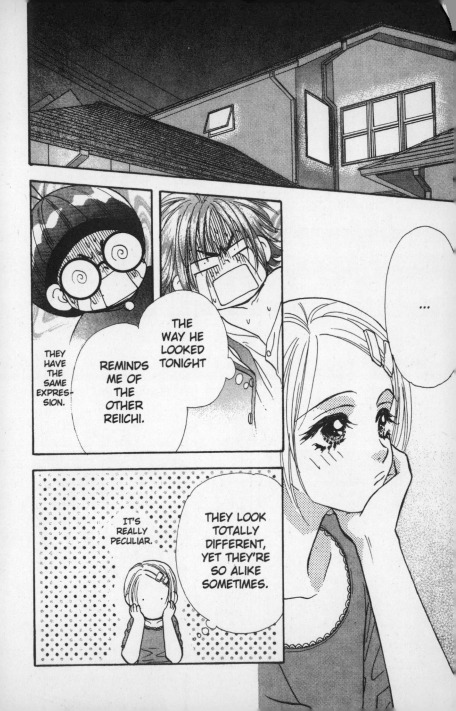

THE WAY HE LOOKED TONIGHT

REMINDS ME OF THE OTHER REIICHI.

THEY HAVE THE SAME EXPRESSION.

...

THEY LOOK TOTALLY DIFFERENT, YET THEY'RE SO ALIKE SOMETIMES.

IT'S REALLY PECULIAR.

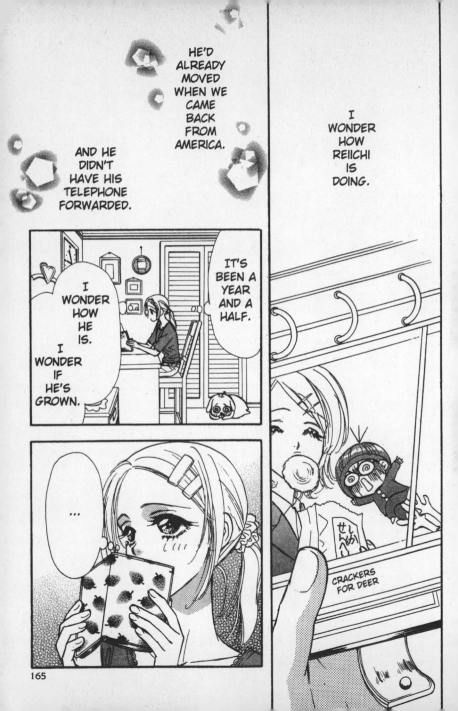

HE'D ALREADY MOVED WHEN WE CAME BACK FROM AMERICA.

AND HE DIDN'T HAVE HIS TELEPHONE FORWARDED.

I WONDER HOW REIICHI IS DOING.

I WONDER HOW HE IS. I WONDER IF HE'S GROWN.

IT'S BEEN A YEAR AND A HALF.

...

CRACKERS FOR DEER

BEEP
BEEP
BEEP
RRRRINGGG
HEY AKI. HOW ARE YOU?
IT'S BEEN A LONG TIME.
I WAS WONDERING IF YOU KNOW ANYONE WHO MIGHT HAVE REIICHI SWAN'S PHONE NUMBER.
...
JOLT
日本アマレ
JAPAN AMATEUR WRESTLING

ALL-JAPAN AMATEUR-WRESTLING
大日本アマレズ
pee
BECOME A MEMBER.
GO TO THE OLYMPICS
AMATEUR WRESTLING

REIICHI'S OUT LATE.
I BET HE COMES HOME IN THE MORNING AGAIN.
MOM, YOU BETTER BAKE ANOTHER CAKE FOR TOMORROW.
OH YES.

めざせ アテネ!

TO BE CONTINUED

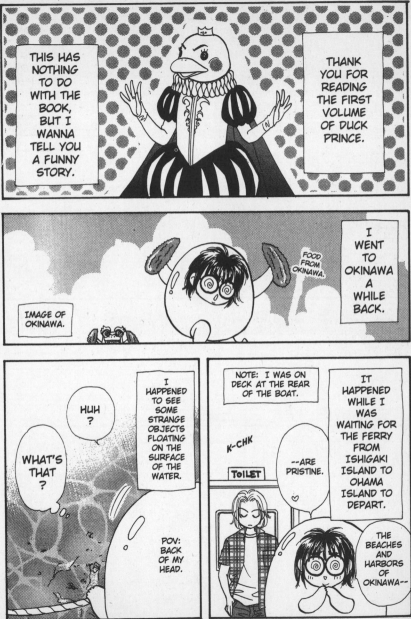

THANK YOU FOR READING THE FIRST VOLUME OF DUCK PRINCE.

THIS HAS NOTHING TO DO WITH THE BOOK, BUT I WANNA TELL YOU A FUNNY STORY.

I WENT TO OKINAWA A WHILE BACK.

FOOD FROM OKINAWA.

IMAGE OF OKINAWA.

I HAPPENED TO SEE SOME STRANGE OBJECTS FLOATING ON THE SURFACE OF THE WATER.

HUH?

WHAT'S THAT?

POV: BACK OF MY HEAD.

NOTE: I WAS ON DECK AT THE REAR OF THE BOAT.

K-CHK

TOILET

--ARE PRISTINE.

IT HAPPENED WHILE I WAS WAITING FOR THE FERRY FROM ISHIGAKI ISLAND TO OHAMA ISLAND TO DEPART.

THE BEACHES AND HARBORS OF OKINAWA--

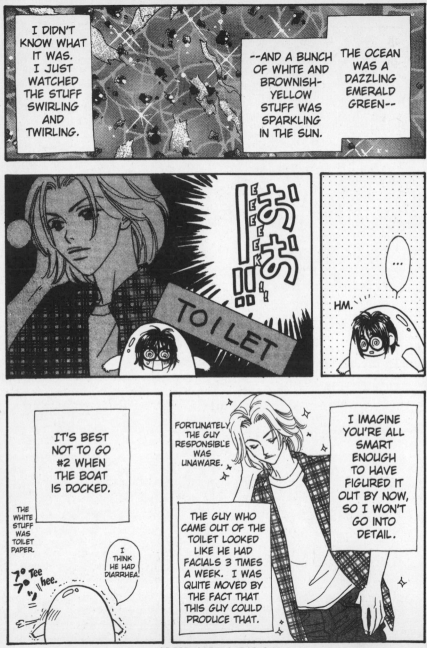

I DIDN'T KNOW WHAT IT WAS. I JUST WATCHED THE STUFF SWIRLING AND TWIRLING.

--AND A BUNCH OF WHITE AND BROWNISH-YELLOW STUFF WAS SPARKLING IN THE SUN.

THE OCEAN WAS A DAZZLING EMERALD GREEN--

TOILET

HM.

...

IT'S BEST NOT TO GO #2 WHEN THE BOAT IS DOCKED.

THE WHITE STUFF WAS TOILET PAPER.

I THINK HE HAD DIARRHEA.

Tee hee.

FORTUNATELY THE GUY RESPONSIBLE WAS UNAWARE.

THE GUY WHO CAME OUT OF THE TOILET LOOKED LIKE HE HAD FACIALS 3 TIMES A WEEK. I WAS QUITE MOVED BY THE FACT THAT THIS GUY COULD PRODUCE THAT.

I IMAGINE YOU'RE ALL SMART ENOUGH TO HAVE FIGURED IT OUT BY NOW, SO I WON'T GO INTO DETAIL.

AFTERWORD * THE END

せんべい

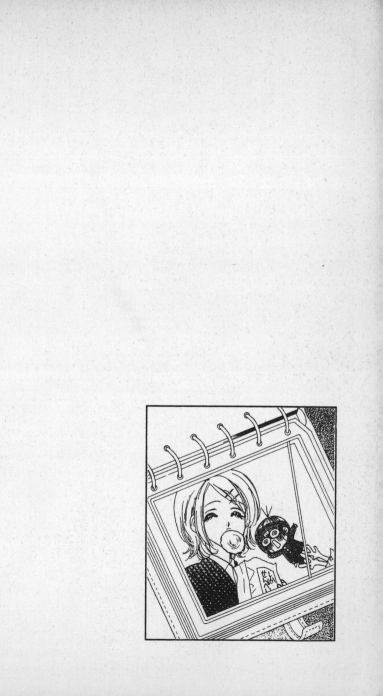

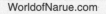